40 YEARS IN THE WILDERNESS:

HOW THE CHURCH CAN SUPPORT THOSE WITH HIV/AIDS

J. MARSHALL SHAMELL

FOREWORD BY RAE LEWIS-THORNTON

Judson Press™
DISTINGUISHED PUBLISHERS SINCE 1824
VALLEY FORGE, PA

40 YEARS IN THE WILDERNESS: HOW THE CHURCH CAN SUPPORT THOSE WITH HIV/AIDS

Interior design by Crystal Devine.

Cover design by Anthony Aranha.

Library of Congress Cataloging-in-Publication data

Names: Shamell, J. Marshall, author.
Title: 40 years in the wilderness : how the church can support those with HIV/AIDS / J. Marshall Shamell.
Other titles: Forty years in the wilderness
Description: Valley Forge, PA : Judson Press, [2025] | Includes bibliographical references.
Identifiers: LCCN 2024051416 (print) | LCCN 2024051417 (ebook) | ISBN 9780817018528 (trade paperback) | ISBN 9780817082598 (epub)
Subjects: LCSH: AIDS (Disease)--Pastoral counseling of--Patients--United States. | AIDS (Disease)--Religious aspects--Christianity. | Church work with the sick--United States.
Classification: LCC BV4460.7 .S43 2025 (print) | LCC BV4460.7 (ebook) | DDC 259/.41969792--dc23/eng/20250108
LC record available at https://lccn.loc.gov/2024051416
LC ebook record available at https://lccn.loc.gov/2024051417

Printed in the U.S.A.
First printing, 2025.

DEDICATION

This book is dedicated to the many men, women, and children who lost their battle with Acquired Immune Deficiency Syndrome. May their loved ones, friends, and those individuals for whom they made a positive impact carry their memories in their hearts for generations to come. This book is also dedicated to the millions of men, women, and children who are living with Acquired Immune Deficiency Syndrome and Human Immunodeficiency Virus. May they have an awesome support group that provides them with love, affirmation, and encouragement while they are on this journey of chronic illness.

IN LOVING MEMORY

James Allen Propes, son (1991–2024)

Marion Jasper Shamell, father (1909–2000)

Rodney Mitchell Bethel, brother (1958–2001)

Jasper Parnell Shamell, brother (1967–2023)

CONTENTS

FOREWORD

I've known J. Marshall Shamell for over three decades. We met at the crossroads of our lives with HIV/AIDS, when I was traveling around the country speaking about my personal journey of living with AIDS. He, on the other hand, was still living in secret about his own HIV diagnosis. I believe our meeting was God ordained. That day I was the keynote speaker for a conference held at a hotel where he was employed. Back then, people would often pull me aside after I spoke to disclose their HIV status, just as he did that day.

Those living with HIV/ADS were isolated as much as they were seeking connection, validation and support. This yearning for connection personally resonated because I also lived in isolation after my HIV diagnosis in 1987. The disease was painted so ugly that I feared discrimination. In the first seven years of my diagnosis, I only told seven-eight people. The fear and shame I had about having HIV rested on me like a monkey attached to my back. I held my secret so close that I didn't read any articles or watch television specials about HIV fearing someone would put two and two together. Most Sundays I cried through worship but did not dare tell a soul at my church. While I wanted support, I was not emotionally prepared for rejection or gossip. Interestingly, I never doubted God's love for me. I simply did not feel lovable.

From the beginning of the AIDS pandemic, I heard so many horror stories about rejection. Parents disowned their children, who died in corridors of hospitals while waiting on a room. Funeral homes feared embalming the dead, and pastors refused to give them a Godly home going service—it did not matter if that person or family were long-standing church members. Discrimination touched everyone with HIV, even children. For example, Ryan White, a preteen who contracted HIV through blood products, was kicked out of school. Hysteria took hold, and rumors about Ryan and his mother ran wild in his small Indiana hometown. It did not matter that Ryan had severe hemophilia. The gossip was shameful to say the least. Ryan's mother, Jeanne White Ginder, told me that people actually rumored that Ryan became infected because she was a poor housekeeper. Someone actually peeked in their window to see if it was true. Ryan and his mother became activists to help fight back the cruelty unleashed on them. The same is true for Hydeia Broadbent, a child born with HIV who was removed from a Las Vegas school at age six. Hydeia's insight into the stigma thrust upon her at her young age ushered her into the national spotlight. Isaiah 11:6 says, "and a little child will lead them all," which speaks to the heart of these children's activism.

Into the late 1990s, discrimination against people living with HIV was rampant. The political climate was scary. It took President Ronald Reagan nearly four years to even mention AIDS, and it was only after his friend, actor Rock Hudson, died from AIDS-related complications. Senator Jesse Helms of North Carolina actually sponsored legislation to isolate persons living with HIV/AIDS from the general population.

The stigma around HIV/AIDS began because of facts regarding the illness's discovery. In 1981 the Center for Disease Control (CDC) reported five cases of pneumocystis carinni pneumonia (PCP) in men who were identified as homosexuals. CDC's Mobility and Mortality Weekly Report (MMWR) purported that PCP had been caused by an immune dysfunction acquired through sexual contact. Once the general press reported these details, people were afraid of what they did not understand. As cases rose, primarily in men who had sex with men, it became hard to fight back the stigma. Earnestly, even the first clinical identifier contributed to the stigma. The scientific community referred to the illness as "Gay Related Infections Disease (GRID)" and "Gay Disease." These initial names, coupled with the first cases presenting in homosexual men who often looked like prisoners of war, helped to birth the stigma still prevalent today. As cases increased by the thousands from additional methods of HIV transmission, including injection drug use, breast feeding, mother to child transmission, blood transfusions and yes even heterosexual sex, the named changed to acquired immunodeficiency syndrome (AIDS). It took another two years after CDC's report for the scientific community to identify HIV as the cause of AIDS. GRID then became Human Immunodeficiency Virus (HIV). The HIV antibody test to detect HIV in blood did not come until 1985, and the first treatment followed in 1987. By then the numbers of HIV cases were as staggering as the stigma and discrimination.

I get it—people wanted to believe that HIV/AIDS could never happen to them, and they told themselves that they were different from the people they knew or saw on television with HIV/AIDS. What they meant was they were not gay or sexually promiscuous nor did they use injection drugs. Those perceived differences created a division in people's minds between those who were HIV infected and those who were not infected or those who were possibility at risk for infection. As a result, the blame game took hold and created "good AIDS" and "bad AIDS." Those who contracted HIV through same sex relations, IV drug users, and unmarried women had "bad AIDS," while people infected by blood transfusions or blood products for medical conditions, babies infected by mothers, or wives infected by husbands (and vice versa) had "good AIDS."

Bad AIDS was perceived as a punishment from God. For many Christians, the most basic form of transmission was rooted in sin. This division affected even the most rational people. Tennis champion Arthur Ash, who was infected from a blood transfusion during open heart surgery, kept his status a secret for fear that someone would think he was gay. That was until the press learned he was infected, and Ashe was forced to publicly disclose. Instead of asking how can we help you? We asked how did you become infected? People were forced to defend how they acquired an illness while managing that illness. HIV's emotional weight was like no other illness. While people wanted support, they were not inclined to risk disclosing at the expense of stigma and discrimination.

Judgment, whether real or perceived, influenced who we told and when we told. I often say the secret of living with HIV/AIDS was killing me quicker than the disease. By the time I went public, I was broken. My initial disclosure was after I transitioned to AIDS. Back then the life expectancy was around eighteen months. Since I was dying, I thought it was time to come clean. My story had a good outcome. When I told my mentor Jesse L. Jackson, he simply said, "I loved you before you had AIDS, and I love you with AIDS," and then we prayed. My pastor learned I had HIV from television after I started speaking publicly. He called me to the front of the church one Sunday morning and asked in front of the congregation, "Was that you I saw on television?"

"Yes," I mumbled.

"Keep up the good work," he added, and I went back to my seat, with my head held high. Reverend Evans licensed me as a minister six years later. While my story had a happy ending as did Shamell's, there are thousands of people whose story didn't end as well after disclosing to family, friends, and yes, even pastors. This book highlights just some experiences people have had with the church and living with HIV. It humanizes those living with HIV, but it also illustrates the failure of some pastors to meet the needs of their parishioners.

Responding faithfully to AIDS challenged the very core of what it meant to be Christian. Looming large are questions about how Christians individually and collectively move beyond fear of a disease to minister to those living with the disease. For certain, some churches and pastors got it right from the beginning. In Chicago for example, Jeremiah Wright, who pastored Trinity United Church of Christ and my pastor, Clay Evans, of Fellowship Missionary Baptist Church offered HIV/AIDS ministries by the late 1980s. The Balm In Gilded, a national non-for profit that Shamell highlights in this book, organized the National Week of Prayer for the Healing of AIDS, giving pastors a vehicle to have programs around HIV/AIDS. Noone could challenge that people living with this disease needed prayer. At minimum, HIV/AIDS was mentioned in a church at least once a year.

We have come a long way in the first three decades of this disease. The science behind HIV is long established. We know HIV cannot be transmitted through regular day-to-day living. HIV is not airborne, so you cannot contract HIV through sharing utensils, using the bathroom, drinking water, or eating food behind someone. Today, it is unlikely a person will contract HIV through a blood transfusion because all donated blood is tested before it is circulated.

Medical advancements around HIV are remarkable. An HIV antibody test allows a person to know their status in twenty minutes. With over thirty antiretroviral medications, usually taken as a combination therapy (ART), treatment actually suppresses the replication of HIV. Even more remarkable, a person living with HIV who maintains an undetectable viral load cannot transmit HIV. Likewise, a pregnant woman being treated with HIV cannot transmit the virus to her child. We even have one-pill-a-day options to prevent the transmission of HIV. Recently, HIV research made a significant contribution to the COVID-19 vaccine.

Even with plenty of treatment, HIV is not over. There is still no cure or vaccine. The numbers of new cases have remained steady over the decades, with an increase of the Black and Brown, and young adult populations. Equally disappointing, attitudes around HIV have moved at a much slower pace than science. Deaths have decreased significantly, which means people are living longer with HIV. At the same time, stigma still avails.

We still have work to do, which is why *40 Years in the Wilderness: How the Church Can Support Those with HIV/AIDS* is a timely roadmap for the church. It is a starting point—a pathway to your church's role with your members who are living with HIV. Shamell not only provides practical information on how to address HIV/AIDS but also unpacks theological issues surrounding this debate. He gives examples of what churches have done around HIV and why. No one is suggesting that you become an AIDS activist, but we are asking you to show up for the sick, the rejected, and the broken. Almost five decades of HIV, ask yourself, "Isn't it time to meet the woman at the well?

—Rae Lewis-Thornton, Minister and Activist

PREFACE

Forty years ago, sensitive Black pastors and socially aware clergy on their staffs awakened from a deep sleep to courageously address the AIDS crisis. Allen Temple Baptist Church of Oakland and Brentwood Baptist Church of Houston were among the churches that provided social services to members and nonmembers with AIDS. These two churches also provided housing for persons afflicted with AIDS. Allen Temple, with assistance from Lafayette-Orinda Presbyterian Church, supported the Mother of Peace orphanage in South Africa for children whose parents had died of AIDS. Some other churches were afraid to address this crisis because of the stigma surrounding AIDS and their conservative theology, which embraced conservative gender ideologies. Other churches did not want to address the problem because the disease was more prevalent in certain ethnic communities, and the churches in those communities with upward class and cultural strivings did not want the rejection that accompanied the HIV/AIDS ministry.

J. Marshall Shamell, who interviewed me for his dissertation when he attended United Seminary, is deeply convinced that church members who could not share with their pastors and churches that they had contracted the disease are forced to live in the wilderness. He has a deep love for the diseased, much like the compassion that Jesus had for the lepers he healed. This call on his life to support those with HIV/AIDS has been heavy on his heart for forty years. The Centers for Disease Control reported on July 25, 2024, that 40 million people are currently living with HIV, and tens of millions have died of AIDS-related causes due to damaged immune systems. This wilderness is an ever-present challenge to the church. Church members without drug use or sexual contact have unfortunately contracted the disease through blood transfusions. This book is contemporary and much needed because many churches are unaware of this crisis after forty years.

—J. Alfred Smith Sr., pastor emeritus of Allen Temple Baptist Church in Oakland, California, and professor emeritus at Berkeley School of Theology, Berkeley, California

WORDS OF THANKS AND APPRECIATION

I would like to thank Dr. G. Martin Young for encouraging me to enroll in the Doctor of Ministry program at United Theological Seminary. Under your tutelage, I visualized a new perspective of growing the church without walls in the twenty-first century.

I would like to express thanks to Dr. Alfred Thompson for bringing your unique style and gifts to the Growing Without Walls and Effective Preaching and Stewardship peer group. I would like to thank Dr. Leroy Cothran and the late Dr. Randy Grimes for allowing me the opportunity to complete my matriculation period in the Gardner C. Taylor Scholars: Prophetic Leadership–Social Justice and Political Action focus group.

I am extremely grateful for the continuous support from my beloved pastor and friend, the Reverend Kevin D. Long, for exemplifying the true meaning of a friend, pastor, and big brother. I would like to also extend thanks to the Reverend A. A. W. Motley and the Reverend Reginald Walton for their friendship and support over the years.

I would like to express a special thank you to these special individuals: Rev. Dr. Louis A. Newby, Rev. Dr. Phillip James, Dr. Ann Taylor, Mrs. Mary E. Malone, Rev. Dr. Kenneth Samuels, Rev. Dr. William Flippin Sr., and Rev. Dr. J. Alfred Smith, Sr. Thank you for providing words of encouragement, edits, and suggestions.

I would like to express my thanks to my mother, Lois E. Shamell, and my siblings, Patrick N. Bethel, Gloria J. Bethel,

Lydia Bethel Brim, and Marian A. Shamell. I recognize my nieces, nephews, great-nieces, great-nephews, cousins, and friends who showered me with unconditional love and support.

To my godchildren—Felisha Manley White, Brittney Johnson, Rev. Andre D. Waller, Tiffany A. Clay, Rev. Dr. Diamond Brooks, and Devonte Bowers— I am extremely blessed to have each of you in my life. You have provided me with such joy in your unique ways. I am proud of all your accomplishments and know that God is not finished with you yet. The best is yet to come.

To my extended siblings—Princess Poyntz, Lareka Killebrew, Sahara Newby Meyers, Teresa Newby Acton, DeShanta Edwards, Rhonda Edwards, Benjamin Rhodes, Alicia Barnett Collins, Ashley Barnett, and Lia McCants Smith—I would like to thank you for accepting me into your family and showing me much substantial encouragement and unconditional love.

I give all glory, honor, and praises to God for guiding my life through trials, tribulations, and challenging times. I thank God for not abandoning me when others did.

INTRODUCTION

More than forty years have passed since the Centers for Disease Control (CDC) revealed the first cases of Acquired Immune Deficiency Syndrome (AIDS) in the United States of America. Months after the first appearance in the United States, scientists identified the Human Immunodeficiency Virus (HIV) as the root cause. When the spread of this virus became an epidemic, the medical world came together in search of a cure. During this time, the broader church, with very few exceptions, took the position of condemning individuals who were infected with this virus. During the early days of this epidemic, many churches refused to dispel the stigma surrounding Human Immunodeficiency Virus /Acquired Immune Deficiency (HIV/AIDS). Unfortunately, many people still stigmatize the disease to this day. Members of the clergy use the pulpit to condemn and deliver messages of damnation toward those affected by the disease.

During the initial epidemic period of the virus, society in general needed to learn basic information about how people could be infected with the virus. Society pushed the narrative that this then newly discovered disease was a homosexual illness, even disparaging it as "gay cancer." Because of the early association between HIV/AIDS and the LGBTQ+ community, many clergy claimed the virus was a curse from God.

However, the narrative began to shift when Arthur Ashe and Ryan White went public with their health statuses. The public was made aware that anyone could get the disease because sex was not the only means of transmission. As more information became available and awareness grew, some congregations established Health and Wellness Ministries with the purpose of providing material on HIV/AIDS prevention. There were campaigns that promoted compassion and collaboration with the medical community to find a cure for this disease.

When the infection rate in women began to spike, the CDC promoted a narrative supporting more preventive measures, such as abstinence and safer sex practices. The organization developed more marketing campaigns to inform the public about how the virus can be passed through blood transfusion, and they raised awareness of how many bisexual men (also known as "down low" men) were infecting women with the virus. Safer sex practices and changing blood donation practices helped to slow the spread of the disease. According to the latest statistics from the CDC, more than 1.2 million people in the United States from the age of thirteen and over are living with the HIV virus.[1] Based on these numbers, there is a high probability that every congregation in the United States contains at least one member who is living with the virus or AIDS.

During the early phases of the HIV/AIDS pandemic,[2] people feared being in the presence of an infected person. At the height of this fear, individuals became hesitant about shaking hands or giving hugs. Some refused to allow infected people to come to family and community gatherings. Some families would throw away silverware, glassware, and even bed linen that individuals who were infected with the virus used. Many individuals who were infected with the virus were required to wear latex gloves and even face masks in order to be in certain environments. Society pushed state and federal governments to pass legislation that would require individuals infected with the virus to be placed in quarantine until a cure could be found or until more knowledge of how the virus could be contained, and not transmitted through normal contact, emerged. Because of this great fear surrounding the virus, many infected individuals decided to isolate themselves from society.

Much has changed since the early days of the pandemic. HIV/AIDS no longer leads to certain death, as medical treatments continue to improve. Today, people can live relatively healthy and long lives as modern antivirals can keep HIV from developing into AIDS. HIV has become more of a chronic illness, requiring ongoing treatment. However, the stigma still exists, and people with HIV can still feel isolated, lonely, and misunderstood. What is the role of the church in supporting these individuals?

During weekly worship services worldwide, congregations offer prayers of concern where petitions are made on behalf of those individuals living with chronic illnesses such as cancer, diabetes, and Alzheimer's disease. We also hear prayers of concern for individuals who are on the road to recovery from alcohol and drug addictions. In those prayers, the faithful ask God to provide healing, deliverance, and a full recovery to those individuals. Some places even invite these individuals to the altar where they can be anointed with oil in anticipation and expectation of a healing from the almighty God. However, individuals who are living with HIV/AIDS often feel excluded from these prayer petitions. Is this omission of individuals who are living with the virus done intentionally? Is it possible that many clergy and worship leaders are unaware that individuals who are living with the virus are members of their congregations? Could the pastor's lack of knowledge be because these members have not shared their status?

We, as the church, must dispel the stigmatization and subsequent discrimination of people living with HIV/AIDS. After all, the stigma has its roots in past theological understandings, not just limited scientific knowledge. This book aims to issue a clarion call of awareness to pastors, congregations, and religious organizations at large. To raise awareness, I seek to foreground the cries of individuals who are living with the virus and share their experiences. As you will see throughout this book, these faithful and dedicated members of various congregations are seeking words of hope, love, and affirmation from their religious leaders and fellow congregation members.

In this book, I share information about many of these topics and what the church can do to support people living with HIV/AIDS. I also provide important data about the current perceptions of churches and pastors and offer examples of effective HIV/AIDS ministries. I invite you to revisit scripture to help shape a theological approach that uplifts and supports people living with this virus and offers inspiration for programming that you can implement in your ministry.

Critically, we must recognize that every church has somebody within its midst who is affected by HIV/AIDS, whether that person is a pastor, churchgoer, or lay leader. Every person is touched by this disease in some way by knowing family members or friends who live with HIV. May this book open our hearts and minds to work together to minister to these important children of God.

NOTES

1. "CDC Publishes New HIV Surveillance Reports," Centers for Disease Control and Prevention, accessed 1 October 2024, https://www.cdc.gov/nchhstp/director-letters/cdc-publishes-new-hiv-surveillance-reports.html. (Please note: due to Executive Orders in January 2025, the CDC website has noted possible changes for compliance.)
2. N.B.: When HIV/AIDS was limited to a few countries, it was considered an epidemic in those countries. Since it is present globally, it is considered a pandemic today.

CHAPTER ONE

THE STATE OF HIV/AIDS MINISTRY IN TODAY'S CHURCH

ONE SUNDAY immediately after morning worship services, a concerned church member approached me. "Pastor, can I have a moment of your time?" she inquired. I was a member of this congregation's ministerial staff, and I noticed right away that she had such a disposition of concern on her face. "Sure," I offered. "How can I be of assistance?" We remained in the sanctuary to talk, and she began to share a story about her oldest adult son who was living with HIV.

Her son's case had begun to progress from HIV to AIDS, and her son was falling into depression. She had encouraged him to attend worship services with her, believing that the service would lift his spirits.

Her son refused to attend any church service because he feared that people would look at him differently because of his health condition. He heard many horror stories of individuals living with the virus who had received unfavorable treatment. Among his friends, some individuals had even been asked to leave the church because members did not feel comfortable being in the same space as them.

"Would you call my son and talk with him about it?" the mother asked. "It would be my pleasure," I responded. "Here's my number. Have him call me first."

Within three days, her son called, and we began a dialogue and established a friendship. I remained in contact with the son for a year. Sadly, his health continued to decline. I would visit him in the hospital, which surprised him so much. One visit, he mentioned how the necktie that I was wearing would look good on him. So, I immediately removed the necktie from my neck and presented it to him. He smiled.

A few months later, he transitioned. His mother asked if I would provide words of comfort at his funeral service. This experience with this young man touched me and inspired me to conduct this research. If this young man, who had grown up with a mother of such strong faith and commitment, had these feelings and reluctance of attending church because of his HIV/AIDS status, then more men, women, boys, and girls are out there who feel the same way.

Stories like these inspired me to take a deeper dive into the needs of congregants living with HIV/AIDS. I wondered—what is the state of ministry to individuals like these? What do churches understand about the virus and people living with it? What can be done to ensure that people like my congregant's son feel welcomed in the house of God? To answer these questions, I decided to study these questions at United Theological Seminary (UTS).

Congregants Living with HIV/AIDS: What do they think?

When I was studying at UTS, I took a deep dive into learning more about the state of HIV/AIDS ministries in the church. As part of my research, I surveyed many people regarding their thoughts about HIV/AIDS ministries. A key group of people who participated in my research were individuals living with the virus. I asked them questions about many topics. The results were eye-opening regarding how affected individuals perceive the church:

- *Disclosing Status to Pastors.* Sixty-three percent of individuals who completed the survey stated they had not shared their positive status with their pastor. Only thirty-four percent have shared their positive status with their pastor.
- *Affirming God's Love of Individuals with HIV/AIDS.* Sixty-two percent agree that the church affirms God's love for individuals living with the virus. Thirty-seven percent disagree.
- *Churches Condoning Stigma and Discrimination.* Fifty-two percent agree that churches condone HIV/AIDS stigma and discrimination, while forty-eight percent disagree.
- *The Church as a Support System.* Forty percent do not feel they have any support from their church, twenty-eight percent report some limited support from their church, and thirty-two percent have a strong support system from their church.

Survey respondents who were living with the virus also expressed strong feelings about actions they want to see the church take. They believe churches should:

- *Fight Stigma and Discrimination.* One hundred percent agree that the church should fight HIV/AIDS stigma and discrimination.
- *Provide Spiritual Support.* Ninety-seven percent agree that the church should provide spiritual support to individuals who are living with HIV/AIDS. They also agree that pastors should play a vital role in providing spiritual support to individuals who are living with HIV/AIDS.

The survey also revealed how people who are living with HIV/AIDS feel about their status:

- *Abandonment.* Twenty-five percent feel a sense of abandonment due to their positive status, while seventy-five percent do not feel abandoned by their church.
- *The Virus Is Not God's Punishment.* Eighty-two percent do not believe that the virus is a punishment from God, while three percent believe that it is. Fifteen percent are unsure if it is.

The key takeaway messages from individuals who are living with the virus are: (1) The church continues to play a significant role in the practice of stigmatization and discrimination against people who are infected with HIV/AIDS; and (2) By remaining silent and not actively participating in the fight to end the stigma associated with the virus both in society and religious community, the church neglects its responsibility in ministry. Now that we know a bit more about the perceptions of congregants living with the virus, what do pastors think?

Ministering to People with HIV/AIDS: What do Pastors Think?

In addition to surveying people living with the virus, I asked a group of pastors to participate. The pastors who completed the survey represented churches from various denominations and nondenominational churches. They had congregations with various sizes of membership, ranging from fifty to one thousand. I sought at least fifty responses from members of the clergy. These results showcase how pastors currently support people living with the virus:

- *Personally Knowing Someone with HIV/AIDS.* Fifty-one percent affirmed that they have a family member or friend who is living with HIV/AIDS, while forty-nine percent were unaware if they know someone who lives with the virus.

- *Feel Pastors Should Provide Spiritual Care.* Seventy-two percent strongly agree that pastors should provide spiritual care to individuals who are living with HIV/AIDS.
- *Feel Pastors Should Fight Stigma and Discrimination.* One hundred percent strongly agree that pastors should play a role in the fight against HIV/AIDS stigma and discrimination.
- *Feel Churches Should Speak Out Against Discrimination.* Sixty-seven percent strongly agree that the church should speak against HIV/AIDS stigma and discrimination.
- *Pastors and HIV status.* Eighty-four percent indicated they have tested negative for HIV/AIDS, while twelve percent indicated they have a positive HIV/AIDS status. Four percent indicated they are unaware of their status.
- *Pastors and Willingness to Disclose.* Forty-six percent would share their positive status with their congregation, while thirty-two percent are unsure if they would share. Twenty-one percent would not disclose their positive status with their congregation.
- *Creating HIV/AIDS Support Ministries.* Ninety-one percent would endorse the formation or host a HIV/AIDS support group within their congregation.
- *HIV/AIDS Is Not God's Punishment.* Ninety-eight percent do not believe that HIV/AIDS is a punishment from God.

In addition to the survey questions above, I asked some open-ended questions. The pastors provided interesting responses about their theological perspectives on the virus. The following statements are a sampling of different pastors' ideas, showing the wide variety of perspectives held in the ministry regarding HIV/AIDS:

- [It is a] A plague. Like cancer, lupus, and other diseases.

- I must love them just as God has commanded.
- The hurt must come for healing.
- God has the power to heal HIV/AIDS.
- It's a medical issue that does not in any way diminish the individual as a child of God.
- Romans 8:28, "And we know that God causes everything to work together for the good of those who love God and are called according to his purpose for them."
- Everyone is suffering from a terminal disease. Our lifestyle has consequences and innocent victims.
- God is a healer and forgives. It is not a punishment.
- For some who contracted it by unnatural means, it is an abomination. For those who contract it from drug use, we should teach forgiveness.
- The causation of AIDS itself is sin, though its contraction may not be; for example, transfusions.
- It is not a curse because of sinful or abominable behavior and should not be treated as such.
- There are many ways to contract the virus. However, if it is done through same sex, forgiveness and healing are always welcome. God hates the sin, yet he loves the sinner.

In many of these responses, pastors seemed to focus their concerns on healing, perhaps in a miraculous healing sort of way. However, they did not focus as much on spiritual health. Some of them seemed concerned with how a person contracted the disease rather than the care of the person. In good pastoral care practice, what matters more for people with an illness: how they contracted it, or how God is working in their lives now?

However, a few pastors reflected a different understanding in their thinking about people living with HIV/AIDS. As above, the following statements are from a variety of pastors, expressing individual theological ideas about ministering to people with the virus:

- HIV/AIDS is a sickness that causes suffering. Jesus would not shame anyone with HIV/AIDS but would love and care for them. They are children of God. We are to love. Love should compel people to treat people with respect, care and compassion regardless of what is going on in their life. Also, the congregation follows the leader and therefore, the leader should lead in a way that produces an environment of love. If we are not infected, we are affected, for we are the body of Christ that is supposed to bear one another's burdens.
- The church should be a place of support for people who are living with the virus.
- We would not demonize someone with cancer, so why would we impose such views suffering from AIDS? I believe God comes so that we might have life and have it more abundantly. It is the devil who comes to kill, steal, and destroy.
- Jesus cared for, touched, and brought healing to people struggling with various diseases and disenfranchisement. We are called to do the same. Since this is also a matter of social justice, churches need to get involved in the community and the issues people live with. This is what it means to be a Christian.
- My theological position is one of love and compassion for people infected with HIV/AIDS and move people from the stereotypical understanding of people infected by this condition.
- Christ did not care about the social stigma attached to the disease but cared about the infected person. We, too, should model Christ's actions and mimic his behavior.

With the responses listed above, there is a positive tone from pastors who understand the need to focus on exercising the principal teachings of Jesus Christ, which are compassion, love, and affirmation. These responses would appropriately answer the question "What Would Jesus Do?" as it relates to meeting the spiritual needs of individuals who are living with any chronic illnesses. These responses offer encouragement, enlightenment, and edification to parishioners regardless of their status in life.

Churchgoers: What do they think about HIV/AIDS and Ministry?

The third group I surveyed consisted of church attendees. These church members come from various religious traditions, and they play active roles in their church. Some highlights of these individuals' surveys follow:

- *Nearly Half of Churchgoers Are Aware of Someone Who Has HIV/AIDS.* Forty-six percent know of friends or family who are living with the virus, while fifty percent are unaware of friends or family who are living with HIV/AIDS.
- *The Church Has Been Silent.* Eighty-five percent feel that the church has been silent in the fight to prevent the spread of HIV/AIDS. Only fifteen percent do not feel that the church has been silent in the fight to prevent the spread of HIV/AIDS.
- *Congregants Believe the Church Can Help.* Eighty-seven percent agree that the church can dispel the stigma and discrimination against people who are living with HIV/AIDS. Ninety-six percent agree that the church should play a role in offering spiritual support to people who are living with HIV/AIDS. Ninety-five percent agree that the pastor should be more active in providing spiritual support to people who are living with the virus.
- *Most Congregants Do Not Carry the Virus.* Ninety percent of the respondents do not have HIV antibodies

and have never been diagnosed with AIDS. Four percent of the respondents have tested positive for HIV/AIDS. Six percent of the respondents are unaware of their health status.

As with the pastors, I asked the churchgoers some open-ended questions. For example, I asked participants why they feel that the church has been silent in the fight to prevent the spread of HIV/AIDS. Some of their top answers were:

- Assume no member of the congregation has tested positive.
- Congregations are not open to discussing the subject.
- The negative stigma associated with the subject.
- The perception that the virus is a gay issue.
- Lack of knowledge and fear.
- Sex topics are taboo in the church.
- Biblical and denominational teaching on sex and HIV/AIDS.

I also asked respondents to share how their churches support people who are living with HIV/AIDS. Some of the top answers were:

- Church does not offer any support to those living with HIV/AIDS.
- Prayer and agency referrals.
- Provide assistance without appearing obvious.
- Accept them for who they are and not what they have.
- My church has an HIV/AIDS ministry.

The information from these three surveys demonstrates why individuals who are living with the virus keep their status silent from their pastors and fellow churchgoers. Here are some of the reasons that might support their decision to remain silent:

1. Pastors and churchgoers have a lack of knowledge of the latest developments with the virus.
2. Biblical and denominational teaching on sex and HIV/AIDS.
3. Congregations are not open to discussing the subject.
4. Pastors do not feel comfortable addressing the subject topic.
5. Pastors and churchgoers are not sure how to apply biblical principles on the subject.
6. The stigma of HIV/AIDS is still present more than forty years later.

From all these responses, we can see churchgoers and clergy members are well aware of the need for the church to speak out against the stigmatization of individuals living with the virus; however, they are waiting for the pastor to take the lead. What can be done to empower church leadership to support those living with HIV/AIDS more effectively?

Reflection Questions

1. How can your church work to dispel the stigma associated with HIV/AIDS?
2. Is your congregation open to discussing the subject of HIV/AIDS beyond how to prevent the spread of the virus? Why or why not?
3. Evaluate the state of your church's HIV/AIDS ministry. How are you offering services of support to individuals who are living with the virus? If your congregation does not have an HIV/AIDS ministry, what would it take to establish one?
4. Is your church a safe space for individuals living with the virus? Can they share their status with the congregation and be welcomed and affirmed?

CHAPTER TWO

CAN WE TALK?

A THIRTY-EIGHT-YEAR-OLD African American man reflects in his journal:

It was a cold day in December 2004. It was exactly on the 15th day of December, which was my 27th birthday! I thought this was going to be a great day full of celebration until I received a phone call from my primary care physician. My doctor informed me that my blood test had shown positive results for HIV. Receiving this type of news was pure devastation for me . . . again so I thought. Life as I knew it was no more. Fast forwarding to 2010, I decided, after much prayer and fasting, to speak with my pastor. During our conversation, I shared with him my health status of having tested positive for HIV. I am a member of a congregation where the membership is around two or three thousand people. I also serve as an Associate Minister in this church. Therefore, I was extremely nervous about sharing my status with him.

In my conversation, I also mentioned to him my desire to share my positive status with the Singles Ministry in which I actively participated. The sole purpose behind making the announcement was merely to show that "One doesn't look like what one is going through." I wanted to show the church that HIV has many different looks and to kill the stigma that the church has held towards individuals who are HIV positive. Not all individuals who are HIV positive look sick or look like they're dying, but they are living healthy and simple lives as normal human beings. I simply used my status as a platform to educate my church.

The response that I received from my church was overwhelmingly filled with nothing but Love, hugs, and many tears! Sharing my positive status with my pastor and church family helped me more than it helped them. By sharing this information, it gave me a sense of liberation and release from the bondage of judgment and fear of being abandoned.

It has been five years since I shared my news with my pastor and church family. I continue to receive much love and support from them; however, many members stop participating in the single ministry because of being afraid of being associated with an individual who is HIV positive. The stigma surrounding individuals living with the virus is hurtful. In closing, I will say until the Black church faces the reality of the effects HIV/AIDS has on the church, the stigma and discrimination against people with HIV/AIDS will persist, and people living with the virus will remain silent and suffer in pain. The church members need more education on how to empower and express love to individuals living with the virus, whether these individuals are heterosexual or same-gender loving. I just happen to be a preacher who is HIV-positive. HIV doesn't have me, but I have it.

This journal entry demonstrates how wonderful it can be when churches embrace a person living with HIV/AIDS. An embracing and supportive response can be transformative for both the affected individual and the church's ministry. So how do we begin these conversations? Can we talk?

Do We Know What We Don't Know?

At the beginning of my study, I theorized that churches do not discuss HIV/AIDS because many church leaders lack knowledge about the virus. The survey results affirmed that idea. Additionally, many clergy and congregation members are still under the mistaken belief that the virus can be contracted through hugging, drinking from the same cup, and blood transfusions. Unfortunately, many individuals refuse to attend HIV/AIDS educational courses, which provide the history and accurate information about how the virus is contracted, what preventive measures are available, and how medical treatment has turned what was once a death sentence into a long-living chronic illness. When clergy and parishioners do not have accurate knowledge of the virus, they may not understand why they need to show compassion and empathy to those who are infected with the virus.

When people are informed that their blood tests reveal HIV or AIDS, their lives are changed forever. Many questions cloud the person's mind: Are the test results correct? Can another test be taken for accuracy? How will I share this news with my spouse/significant other? What am I going to do? Can this really be happening to me? God, why me? As they leave the doctor's office, the physician may present them with counseling information, but the individuals are left to start a new chapter in their lives on their own. As the news sinks into their minds and thoughts, they must decide who to tell first. Will they share this news with their significant other, best friend, or family member, or will they tell their pastor/spiritual advisor? Once they have decided whether to share this information, the next question they might ask is what type of counseling care can help them cope with this dramatic and life-changing revelation.

From this moment, their decisions about how to proceed and to whom they turn for this type of care will have a lasting impact on their lives. The right type of counseling and care can encourage an individual to look at the diagnosis in a positive manner and not as a death sentence. The wrong type of counseling or care session can steer an individual into a downward spiral of hopelessness.

In many instances, when individuals are wrestling with the vicissitudes of life, they seek guidance, counseling, and solace. In African American culture, people have been taught to bring these concerns to God in prayer and to the elders of the church. For generations, the fellowship of the church has served as an extended family. Most importantly, the church is the place where people are accepted and loved regardless of their issues. However, since the virus's appearance, the church has turned its head and closed its ears to the concerns and supplications of those living with it. This lack of concern and compassion for these groups of people has caused people living with the virus to question their faith in God and doubt the sincerity of the church's objectives.

The Church and Healing

Saint Augustine purportedly once said, "The church is not a hotel for saints; it is a hospital for sinners."[1] If we are to embrace the hospital metaphor for the church, we understand it to mean that individuals have the opportunity to bring any sickness to the church in order to seek healing. For many years, most hospitals did not deny services from anybody regardless of illness or ability to pay for services. Perhaps that was once true of the church as well. After 1981, church administrators seemingly changed their policies. After the HIV/AIDS epidemic came to light, churches, at least tacitly, made the decision to only meet the needs of congregants who are not infected with the virus. More than forty years later, this stance remains in place in many churches throughout the United States and throughout the world.

Early in the HIV/AIDS epidemic, the general public thought that HIV/AIDS was the result of a homosexual lifestyle, which some in the Christian world believed an abomination unto God due to the use of a few translations of scripture. For this reason, some people assume that this disease is God's punishment for those individuals who choose to practice this alternative lifestyle. However, several years later, when a number of new cases were identified, representing children, heterosexual women, and seniors (both male and female above the age of sixty-five), there was a shift away from interpreting the virus as God's punishment. While people may have moved away from interpreting HIV/AIDS as God's punishment, they continued to move toward the practice of stigmatization and non-affirmation of people living with it.

Too many churches fail to provide a ministry of compassion for those individuals who were infected with this life-changing disease. The spirit of abandonment is ever-present when a church refuses to open its doors to families who were planning funeral services or memorial services for individuals whose death is classified as an HIV/AIDS-related death. Families would isolate and disassociate themselves from their loved ones because of the virus. Even while being discriminated against and stigmatized by the church, people living with HIV/AIDS continue to come to church worship service in order to hear God's word and seek affirmation of God's love toward them. What churches have risen up to answer that call for people with HIV/AIDS? What inspired them to engage in such a ministry?

A Pastor Makes a Difference

On Wednesday, October 21, 2014, the Reverend Dr. J. Alfred Smith Sr., pastor emeritus of Allen Temple Baptist Church in Oakland, California, shared a story with a group of clergy members who were participating in the doctor of ministry program at United Theological Seminary in Dayton, Ohio. He spoke about how his personal physician made a request to meet with him and several other pastors in the Oakland area. Smith recalled that during this conversation, the physician stated, "Several of your congregation members' deaths were not caused by cancer. The family and the deceased used 'cancer' as a way to disguise the truth; they were infected with HIV/AIDS. To many of these individuals, I served as their physician and pastor. To all of you pastors, I am tired of doing your job. I can't continue to be their physician and pastor. I need for each of you to start doing your job."

At that moment, Smith decided that Allen Temple would create an HIV/AIDS ministry. The life-changing conversation with this physician took place around 1985, and in 1987, the congregation supported Smith's recommendation to establish an HIV/AIDS ministry. Smith recognized that, due to the stigma associated with being infected with HIV/AIDS, many individuals still have to live a life full of discretion and falsehood in order to shield themselves and their families from negative and judgmental attitudes from a place where they should receive the spirit of love and refuge during their time of need.

Smith recognized that the church needed to dramatically change its theology and actions to meet the needs of these children of God. It was time to talk about it. We will continue to learn about Allen Temple and other churches and how they have transformed their ministry to support those living with HIV/AIDS. His church family realized, guided by his leadership, that it was time to open the conversation about ministering to people with HIV/AIDS. Perhaps your church family is facing a similar reckoning. What theological assumptions do you hold as you consider how to minister to people with HIV/AIDS? I invite you to consider your beliefs through the following questions.

Reflection Questions

1. Put yourself in the shoes of a recently diagnosed person. If you were to receive an HIV-positive test result, what Christian principle or phrase do you think would help remove the fear and anxiety? Why?
2. If a family member disclosed their status to you, what theological principle would you share to provide hope and a positive outlook? Why?

3. What Bible verses do you think of when you think about Jesus' healing ministry? How can Matthew 25: 1-13 be applied to meeting the needs of individuals who are living with the virus?

NOTE

1. Greg Schuelter, "Mass Confusion: 'Church as Hospital for Sinners'" in Catholic 365, accessed July 31, 2024, https://www.catholic365.com/article/6821/mass-italicize-mass-confusion-church-as-hospital-for-sinners.html.

CHAPTER THREE

CRIES FROM THE WILDERNESS

The Merriam-Webster Dictionary defines *wilderness* as:

1. a (1): a tract or region uncultivated and uninhabited by human beings
   (2): an area essentially undisturbed by human activity together with its naturally developed life community
   b: an empty or pathless area or region
   c: a part of a garden devoted to wild growth
2. obsolete: wild or uncultivated state
3. a: a confusing multitude or mass: an indefinitely great number or quantity
   b: a bewildering situation

People who receive an HIV/AIDS diagnosis often enter a wilderness phase. This phase becomes most apparent during moments when they feel alone. They are scared because they are unsure of their surroundings being in this wilderness area of life. The wilderness feels filled with wild animals. The temperature is cold. The atmosphere is wet and gray. Most importantly, being in the wilderness makes people feel isolated in this world. Navigating life becomes challenging after receiving this type of life-changing diagnosis because it is filled with many unknowns.

In the early years of the HIV/AIDS pandemic, no drug regime had been established or approved by the Federal Drug Administration. Effective treatments started to arrive in the early 1990s. Life expectancy for individuals with the virus was between two to seven years, and many health insurance companies would not accept patients with this condition, as it was deemed a "pre-existing condition." When President Obama signed the Patient Protection and Affordable Care Act (also known as the Affordable Care Act/ACA) in 2010, the program provided hope to millions of citizens who were living with the virus. Finally, they would not be denied coverage due to their pre-existing condition. The Affordable Care Act was a blessing to those individuals living with HIV/AIDS because they were finally guaranteed access and insurance coverage to proper medical care and prescriptions.

Still today, the many unknowns in the lives of people living with HIV/AIDS cause them additional anxiety, stress, and worry. Many individuals living with the virus express that they desperately want to reach out to a religious leader or spiritual advisor for guidance, assistance, and a sense of direction. However, finding a compassionate religious leader or spiritual advisor can be particularly challenging, contributing to a sense of being lost in the wilderness. This wilderness state of mind causes individuals living with the virus to wonder if and when they would ever depart from this isolating, empty state of being and enter a space of peace, liberation, and clarity.

Individuals who are living with the virus are just like other churchgoing people who seek a ministry of presence when facing life-threatening illness. As we hear in the stories that follow, individuals who are living with the virus desire for members of their religious communities to share with them scripture passages, songs of inspiration, or even words of encouragement. A meaningful visit with a clergyperson or lay leader can bring them out of the mindset of hopelessness or depression and help them obtain an attitude of positivity, prosperity, and productivity.

Daily, individuals who live with HIV/AIDS feel cut off from others and the world. Many of these individuals do whatever is necessary to keep their health statuses silent. They fear being isolated from their coworkers, friends, fellow students, families, and church families. The church is filled with worshippers who strive to live a life that is similar to the life of Jesus Christ and live out the principles of the man who they call Messiah. The house of worship should be a place where individuals come to receive words of encouragement through a sermonic message, to be uplifted by the musical selections rendered by the choir or soloist, to offer up prayers of acknowledging the presence and existence of God, and to confess their sins and shortcomings to the Holy Trinity. They offer thanksgiving for being spared another week of life. They offer thanksgiving for being offered grace and mercy when they should have received justice and damnation. Congregants submit themselves to the will of the Creator with their hearts, souls, and minds.

Instead, most people who are living with HIV/AIDS attend a church where the pastor, other church officials, and members are unaware of their statuses. So, they attend church on a weekly basis, hurt, confused, and seeking comfort from their church family but fear revealing their statuses in fear of judgment and rejection from them. This is where the wilderness clashes with the wildlife. There are voices of individuals who are living with either HIV or AIDS who are crying out in the wilderness, searching for a word of encouragement, inspiration, and most importantly, affirmation of God's love from the wildlife around them. They desire to learn that God has neither abandoned nor forsaken them but that because of their acceptance of God's only begotten son, Jesus Christ, they will inherit eternal life. Their health status or condition will not eliminate them from receiving eternal life.

It is important to listen to the voices of individuals who are living with HIV or AIDS. What can they tell us about their lived experiences from sharing their positive status with their pastor and church family? In what ways had those who had disclosed their status to their church had their pastor and church family supported them? What about those who had not disclosed their status? What were their experiences of continued participation in church life? I share some of their stories in the following pages.

A FORTY-YEAR-OLD AFRICAN AMERICAN MAN

My experience coming out positive was a pleasant one. I found out my status in September of 1995. At that point, I didn't belong to any church. A few months later, I united with a Baptist church here in Atlanta that wasn't affirming, so I didn't feel comfortable discussing my status with anyone there. I attended that church for five years off and on until I met my current partner, and he invited me to Bible study at his church, which was an affirming church. It just so happens that I knew the pastor's partner from many years before that. The pastor's partner also did a lot of work in HIV/AIDS prevention and treatment. He, my partner, and I were talking, and I shared my status with him.

At that point, our ministry didn't have an HIV/AIDS ministry, so together we started one at the church. We had several meetings where people who were dealing with HIV/AIDS and those who were affected by the disease in any way attended. We also have speakers come and address the congregation on World AIDS Day each year. The ministry was operative for three years, until the ministry was dissolved. Although, I still feel that the subject is taboo. Even in a congregation where a high percentage of members are same-gender loving and where the pastor and most of the leadership are same-gender loving, there is a lack of interest in providing education on the subject of HIV/AIDS and help dispel the stigma and discrimination of the virus in the church. In my opinion, people would rather focus on prosperity rather than healing or prevention.

A Fifty-six-year-old Caucasian Woman from Cape Town, South Africa

I was divorced for ten years when I met my late husband. We met in January of 2008 and were married in June of 2008. At the time of our union, he was twelve years my senior. In 2010, after returning from a holiday trip, my husband became sick. He was losing weight drastically from March to June for no apparent reason. He went to the hospital in an attempt to diagnose the reason for the weight loss.

After several tests were performed on my husband, the doctor informed me that my husband's test results revealed the presence of Acquired Immunodeficiency Syndrome. At the time of the diagnosis, his CD4 count was as low as 4—a sign of a severely weakened immune system. I had to disclose the results to my husband. He first denied the results. After taking him home, he refused to take any of the medication. I took care of him to the best of my ability for eleven years until his transition. After his death in 2011, I came to learn that my blood test result showed the presence of HIV antibodies. After learning the news of his health status, I shared the news with our friends and family. Unfortunately, many of our friends disassociated themselves from us in fear and lack of knowledge of how the virus is transmitted. Another reason why they kept their distance from us is because of the stereotype and stigma that comes with the virus.

In 2012, my son was killed in an automobile accident, which has caused me additional hurt and pain. I am in an area where medical treatment is hard to obtain and is very expensive. My husband and I went to church weekly, but it felt like people came to church just to see what a person infected with AIDS looked like, and they were not concerned about how we were feeling. Each Sunday after leaving church, we felt that the pastor and congregation didn't care about us. Prior to my husband's death, we stopped attending church.

I continue to read my Bible daily, but I have not returned to any church building.

A Thirty-year-old African American Woman

I found out I was HIV positive in February 2009. I rarely spoke with the bishop or pastor (who are husband and wife) of my church. I had only been a member of the congregation for a few months when I received my diagnosis.

One day, I finally gained the courage to call the bishop to share my health status. Upon sharing the news with the bishop, I was surprised to hear him immediately tell me it would work out fine, and HIV would not kill me. To receive this type of encouragement and support from my spiritual leader was uplifting. After the initial conversation between the bishop and me, we did not discuss it much; however, the bishop allowed me to be a liaison for an HIV and health ministry.

One year later the bishop was convicted by the Spirit of God to allow members in the HIV and health ministry to share their stories before the congregation during a Sunday early morning worship service. The bishop has embraced members of the congregation who are living with HIV/AIDS. He feels that a pastor who does not openly accept those who are living with the virus has a selfish heart.

My Story

My personal story began on the day I received the news that I had tested positive for the Human Immunodeficiency Virus. It took several years for the news to register in my mind. I attempted to erase the news from my memory, but unfortunately, for the first year and half, I was reminded of my diagnosis when I had to travel for my medical evaluation. The fortunate part was that I was in the military, which allowed me to receive the best medical care during that time. Physically, I was in excellent health but mentally in a state of shock and denial. A personal relationship with God prevented me from committing suicide. The spiritual foundation that had been laid in my life at an early age allowed me to rest on the promises of God. I personally believed that God would not leave me, nor would God forsake me, especially during this critical time in my life.

On that evening of receiving my diagnosis, I made a decision to live and not die. I wanted to beat the odds of living with the virus, so I prayed to God, requesting that I reach the age of fifty. In my mind, being the age of twenty-four and living to reach the age of fifty, with the help of God, I would have beaten the odds of living with the virus. During this period that I first lived with the virus, life expectancy of individuals was seven years. After receiving the news of my diagnosis, I went through a period of isolation. I became inactive in the church, and I began to question my existence. I was disappointed that I would never have the chance of having additional children and getting married. My self-esteem dropped to the lowest point in my life—an all-time low. I walked away from using my gift of choral direction and fulfilling my call to the preaching of the Gospel. I just lost my joy!

Through that period of time, I received words of encouragement from the former North Carolina State Wolfpack Men's Basketball Coach, Jimmy Valvano. He was suffering with cancer, and the doctors had given him a certain amount of time to live. During the 1993 ESPY Award, he made the following statement, which had a lasting impression on my life and provided me with the encouragement to live and not die. He said these words: "I may have cancer, but cancer doesn't have me. Don't ever give up, don't you dare ever give up." The words of televangelist Robert Schuler also inspired me, which I continue to use to this day as motivation to live; "Tough times never last; but tough people do." One day the Lord directed me to the scripture reference of 2 Corinthians 4:8-10 (NLT), which reads, "We are pressed on every side by troubles, but we are not crushed; We are perplexed but yet not in despair. We are hunted down but never abandoned by God. We get knocked down, but we are not destroyed. Through suffering, our bodies continue to share in the death of Jesus so that the life of Jesus may also be seen in our bodies."

I took this motto as my ticket to move forward in life and live. For more than twelve years, I lived life without disclosing my health status to my congregation. Even serving as an associate minister at several churches throughout the United States, I did not feel comfortable sharing my status with the pastor or any congregation members. I had experienced abandonment before on a personal level, so I did not want to experience abandonment from my church family. I revealed my status to my church family during a worship service experience while I was delivering the morning sermon. Some members of the congregation embraced me with love and support, while others did not express any reactions. There were some members who refused to touch my hand or embrace me with a hug. The pastor of the congregation offered support and continued to provide love. By sharing my status with the congregation, I felt a sense of liberation. I regained my self-esteem, which allowed me to live a healthier and positive life.

Three years later, while delivering a sermonic message, I shared my positive status from the pulpit for the first time. At the end of the service, a listener whispered in my ear that he appreciated the message. He resonated with the content of the message because he was living with HIV. He had been struggling to accept the diagnosis, and for the first time, he felt encouraged and enlightened. After spending time with this listener over the following five to six months, I began to think about how many other individuals who are living with the virus are suffering in silence. There are other individuals who are crying out loud seeking affirmation from God and from the church. He and I were both desiring to hear from God's messengers that God will not nor has not abandoned us because of our infection with this virus.

Will the body of Christ follow in the footsteps of John the Baptist to pave a way for individuals who are living with the virus to receive the words, the anointing, and the power of God, so they can live life and live life more abundantly?

My Personal Journal

In addition to my story above, I share some excerpts from my personal journal to show what goes through the mind of an individual who is living with HIV. How does this virus affect people like me mentally, emotionally, physically, and spiritually? How does an individual tend not to allow the positive diagnosis to become a negative burden on their life? I took the time to chronicle some thoughts where I highlight the following items: (1) Living in silence with the virus; and (2) The fear of having my diagnosis disclosed.

JOURNAL ENTRY #1

Dear Journal,
Living life as being HIV positive can be very challenging mentally. Once you received the diagnosis from the doctor of your positive status, your mind began to run with many thoughts like: Who will I tell? Will I tell anyone? How long is my life expectancy? I don't feel sick, so how can I have this virus? Why didn't the person who infected me tell me of having the virus? Why did I let my guard down? Is this a dream? Perhaps when I take the second test, the results will be negative. The doctor just told me that I am HIV positive. Oh God help me!!

For more than several weeks, the above questions continued to rumble in my head, which affected me in keeping focus on the other things of life. I would attempt to place these thoughts in the back of my mind but wasn't successful. I cried day and night. I cried myself to sleep and attempted to ignore what the doctor told me. The way that I took this news was like receiving the death news of someone who was close to me. I was straight in denial. I would pray each night like Paul asking for this thorn to be removed. I believed that God would perform a miracle by the time I went back for a follow-up doctor's appointment.

Unfortunately, when I went back and received the test results, I was informed that I was positive. When the doctor shared what recommended treatment plan, I really wasn't paying attention. The doctor continued to state that I would have to come into the office every six months to check the blood level and CD4 count and see how my body is accepting the medication. To be honest, I wasn't paying attention. I was spaced out. After receiving the prescription, I initially threw the paper away. I had made a decision to not take the medication. It took me more than a year to mentally accept the news of my positive status. I started the medication treatment plan but after two years, I stopped the regime. When my CD4 count began to decrease, I started the medication treatment plan again. I wasn't consistent in taking the medication, so after another two years, I stopped the medication treatment plan. My numbers would play a roller coaster, and the medical team warned me that if I keep starting and stopping taking the medication, my body will start rejecting the medication in general, and I opened myself to opportunistic disease. So, I went home and offered this prayer unto God.

"Dear God, I thank you for life. I come before you bringing unto you this diagnosis of HIV positive. I have made several requests for you to remove the diagnosis, but you reminded me that your grace is sufficient. I didn't listen to your words, so this burden continues to be in the forefront of mind. So, now I come before you requesting to move this burden to the back of my mind. Allow me the opportunity to totally trust you and not allow my status to control me. Instill in me this phrase, 'I may have HIV, but HIV will not have me.' Remind me to repeat to myself this new phrase, Hallelujah, I'm Victorious and that's positive. I offered this prayer in Jesus' name. Amen."

From that night of offering this prayer, I began to live life, and I am living life more freely and not being burdened with thoughts of this health status controlling my life. It was from that night, I took control of my mental handling of this virus and took control of how I would use this positive status as the motivation to live with a positive attitude, positive outlook and knowing that positive things will happen in my life. Years later my accomplishments in my careers have been a result of me having a positive attitude.

JOURNAL ENTRY # 2

Dear Journal,
For many years, I was in the state of denial of my status and did my hardest to keep my status private, especially from my parents. With the negative stigma that is associated with this virus, I never wanted my parents to be bothered with any backlash. I was very selective with whom I shared my status. With this important information, I couldn't trust any and everybody for fear of someone disclosing my status to my parents. However, on several occasions, my status was shared with other people without my consent, which caused me to be very angry. The reason for keeping my status private is not based on being ashamed. After many years of being in denial, I finally accepted responsibility for my actions and how my lack of decision caused me to have this incurable disease. I also came to the reality that I couldn't continue to beat myself and allow this spirit of guilt and disappointment to control my life. But I wanted to be the person to share my status, at my time and to whom I deemed necessary. I can't lie, which is another reason why I didn't want to share my status with the entire world. I wasn't ready to answer the question, "How did you become infected?" and I didn't want to be rejected and abandoned by the church, family, and friends.

When the virus first hit society, many states and localities passed legislation that required individuals who were infected with the virus to share their status with their partners if they engaged in unprotected intercourse. It was during this infancy of the virus when medication had not yet been developed to surpass the virus. This new legislation would charge an individual with "attempted murder" or "assault to commit bodily harm with a dangerous weapon." With a conviction on these charges, prison sentences range from two years to life in prison without the possibility of parole.

Forty years later and with medical progress, the medication now consists of three drugs located in one pill. With this advancement in medical science, these new medications keep the virus so low that the virus is undetectable. When an individual has been medically classified as "undetectable," it means that the virus can't be passed to another individual by exchanging bodily fluids. Even with this advancement in medical science, individuals who are infected with the virus must share their status with their partners prior to engaging in unprotected intercourse. I am grateful to God for allowing scientists to develop such medical treatments that assist individuals who are living with the virus to possibly have some longevity of productive life. When the virus first appeared, life expectancy for people living with the virus was seven years. Now there are individuals who have been living with the virus for more than thirty-five years. Again, thank you God for leading these scientists to develop this new medical treatment.

I must admit and find it very challenging and difficult as an individual who is living with the virus to enter into a relationship. The hard part is to determine at what part of the courtship I should tell the individual of my status. I have shared the status at the beginning of the courtship, and I have shared the status in the middle of the courtship. I never waited until the courtship became a committed relationship before sharing the status. Regardless, when the status is shared, the risk of the individual rejecting being in a relationship with you is present.

Many individuals are uncomfortable with being in a relationship with someone who is living with the virus because they lack knowledge and education about the virus. Many of them are still reflecting on the information that was distributed back in the mid-1980s but have not received the latest education about how the course of the virus and medical science has progressed over the last forty years. Even if the person who is living with the virus offers to provide information and even the physician's contact information, the individual refuses to receive it. Unfortunately, that is the hardest part of being an individual who is living with the virus. Rejection of any kind is never an excellent thing. Being rejected is a reminder of how my lack of conscience and irresponsible decision as a younger person had a negative impact on my life in my later years. I tried to encourage myself by remembering that this is not the person who I need to be with if they can't accept me. But also, it is not fair to place them in such a dilemma. I continue to remind myself to keep in mind the thoughts of the individual and try not to be selfish. The desire to be in a committed relationship is important and being in a happy and committed relationship with someone who has mutual feelings for you is more than important.

So, Journal, I, at times, take on the mindset of the Apostle Paul; I am content in whatever state I am in. If I remain single or am in a committed relationship, I am content. However, there are times when loneliness is very heavy and can bring a low in spirit. Yes, the Lord is always with me, and the Holy Spirit is also present but having companionship would be very nice. If the Lord's will, a special person will enter into my life to be that companion and lover. Until then, I will continue to have a positive attitude, a positive outlook, and a smile on my face.

Conclusion

Individuals who have been living with the virus for a long period of time must now add to their concern the potential of being diagnosed with another chronic illness. A news article on HIV.gov states:

> People aging with HIV share many of the same health concerns as the general population aged 50 and older: multiple chronic diseases or conditions, the use of multiple medications, changes in physical and cognitive abilities, and increased vulnerability to stressors. In addition, while effective HIV treatment has decreased the likelihood of AIDS-defining illnesses among people aging with HIV, many HIV-associated non-AIDS conditions occur frequently in older persons with HIV, such as cardiovascular disease, diabetes, renal disease, and cancer. These conditions are likely related to a number of interacting factors, including chronic inflammation caused by HIV. Researchers are working to better understand what causes chronic inflammation, even when people are being treated with ART. HIV and its treatment can also have effects on the brain. Researchers estimate that between 25 and 50 percent of people with HIV have HIV-Associated Neurocognitive Disorder (HAND), a spectrum of cognitive, motor, and/or mood disorders categorized into three levels: asymptomatic, mild, and HIV-associated dementia. Researchers are studying how HIV and its treatment affect the brain, including the effects on older people living with HIV.[1]

These new potential medical conditions add to the concern of if and when the virus will begin to destroy body organs, which could cause major health concerns and long periods of suffering and pain. It is more important for an individual who is living with the virus to be able to find some form of solace, peace, and tranquility. However, as is obvious in so many stories, the stigma of being diagnosed with the virus in the twenty-first century is still present and the lack of compassion to those individuals who are infected with the virus.

Reflection Questions

1. How have these stories challenged your thoughts and perception of individuals who are living with HIV/AIDS?
2. Do these stories remind you of someone you know who is living with the HIV virus or who has died from AIDs-related disease, or how do they resonate with you if you are not aware of someone who has lived with it?
3. If you were living with HIV/AIDS, would you consider remaining single, or would you seek a committed relationship? Why?

Note

1. "Aging with HIV," HIV.gov, https://www.hiv.gov/hiv-basics/living-well-with-hiv/taking-care-of-yourself/aging-with-hiv.

CHAPTER FOUR

BAD THEOLOGY KILLS

When our African ancestors were brought to this undeveloped land to build a country that would become the greatest, most populous, richest, and most powerful country in the world, slave owners would use manipulation, brainwashing, and punishment to control these workers. These unwilling workers from Africa were very skillful, educated, and intelligent beings. The slave owners were aware of the level of spirituality these individuals had. The slave owners witnessed the enslaved people's worship experience and how these groups of people placed their hope, trust, and faith in God. In order to ensure the enslaved people would be obedient and conform to the method of submission, the slave owners instilled two important things: 1. Do not question the commands and orders of white people, and 2. Do not question God.

For more than four hundred years, the African American community has passed down the idea of never questioning God from generation to generation. The slave owners understood our ancestors would steal away in the Hush Harbors to have a little conversation with God. They did not want their servants to ask God the questions found in Psalm 13:

1. How long will you forget us? Forever?
2. How long will you look the other way?

3. How long must we struggle with anguish in our souls, with sorrow in our hearts every day?
4. How long will our enemy have the upper hand?

The slave owners knew that God heard and answered prayers, and that God would protect and allow no harm to come upon his people. Finally, the slave owners predicted if the servants called on God, God would deliver them from this bondage, and they would no longer have their free labor.

This slave owner mandate for enslaved people to not question their orders lest they question God had a long-lasting impact and is an example of a "bad theology" intentionally taught to a group of people. This bad theology had a negative impact on the African American community for centuries. We were not allowed to ask God why terrible things were happening to us. We were not allowed to know God's desire for us as it related to achieving our full potential. From the times when husbands were separated from their wives and children to wives being separated from their children, our community was under the impression that this type of action was the "will of God," and thus, we accepted it. However, this type of pain could never be relieved, and it undoubtedly caused more early deaths due to poor health conditions. This theology was created by individuals taking scripture verses out of context to push their personal agendas.

Consider again the questions from Psalm 13. People who suffer from chronic diseases, with the complexities and hardships these illnesses bring, also find themselves begging God to respond to their questions. Knowing how bad interpretations impact the lives of individuals in pain, is it not time for us to refrain from spreading bad theology? We need to understand that God accepts our questions, and we need to start encouraging people to go to God with their problems and concerns. We must go to Jesus with all our cares. In the words of songwriter E. A. Hoffman, "I must tell Jesus all of my problems. I cannot bear these burdens alone. In my distress, He will kindly help me. He ever loves and cares for His own."[1]

When Theology Leads to Stigma

What do we mean by the word *theology*? What are some of the theological issues behind the opinions we read in the first chapter? What are some alternative ways we can think about God's will for the church's ministry for people with HIV/AIDS? These questions matter because theology plays a significant role in the treatment of people living with the virus.

According to the *Merriam-Webster Dictionary*, theology is the study of religious faith, practices, and experiences, especially the study of God and the study of God's relations to the world.[2] Owen C. Thomas and Ellen K. Wondra, noted professors of theology, define the field as the following: "Theology is the methodical investigation and interpretation of the content of Christian faith, the orderly clarification and explanation of what the Christian message affirms."[3] One pathway through which Christians form theological beliefs is how they interpret biblical text and how that text resonates from the person's perspective.

An individual's theological foundation is also formed by their parents' teaching, political influences, societal expectations, sermons from their pastor, and their church's dogma. Theology can be expressed and learned through the music genres of Gospel, Christian, and contemporary. The lyrics express the religious and spiritual beliefs of the writer. The writer's message in the song reflects how the composer has been blessed or rescued, or perhaps they are offering an expression of gratitude to the higher being. The late Edward L. Smith, professor of theology at the Interdenominational Theological Center in Atlanta, Georgia, calls this form of theological teaching *embedded theology*, stating, "It is the implicit theology that Christians live out in their work and daily lives."[4] Embedded theology guides individuals throughout their lives.

An individual's theology influences their choices in their careers, their life decisions, and, most importantly, their relationship with God. Identifying and unpacking their embedded theology allows individuals to open dialogue with ministry leaders. Some questions they might seek to address include: Where is God in my life? Is God truly omnipresent? How do I know God is present in my life? As individuals develop through life, they may find many of these questions answered through a more in-depth study of the biblical text, which an individual may conduct on their own. In some cases, individuals gain more understanding of what theology is and how they have applied this term in their lives. Oftentimes, as individuals become more studious of the scripture, their theology will be confirmed or will shift in a different direction. It is so possible for the embedded theology of an individual to change as the individual conducts deeper research and study of the Bible and goes through life's trials and hardships.

For example, prior to my study at the Interdenominational Theological Center, I was taught that women could not be called by God to preach the Gospel. This was part of my embedded theology. Oftentimes, believers would cite 1 Corinthians 14:34 (NKJV), which reads, "Let your women keep silent in the churches, for they are not permitted to speak; but they are to be submissive, as the law also says." With a deeper understanding of the text, I came to understand that this passage of scripture was that women were causing distraction by asking their husbands about the meaning of the message during the worship experience. So, Paul instructed the women not to ask questions during the worship services. If they had any questions regarding the message, they should wait until they returned home and ask their spouses for a clearer understanding. Through this new profound knowledge of the scripture, I learned how this scripture has been misinterpreted to limit the service of women in the church, and my theology changed.

WHAT THEOLOGICAL IDEAS KEEP CHURCHES FROM HELPING?

One theological idea that keeps churches from leading the way in offering compassion to people living with HIV/AIDS is the incorrect idea that the virus is somehow caused by homosexuality. In the minds of some devout Christians, homosexuality and lesbianism are the worst sins against God that can ever be committed. When the public first learned about HIV/AIDS, some leaders and members of the Christian community believed this disease was God's punishment for individuals who practiced this lifestyle. How did this theological idea enter the public consciousness?

On June 5, 1981, the U.S. Center for Disease Control and Prevention (CDC) published a Morbidity and Mortality Weekly Report (MMWR) describing cases of a rare lung infection, *pneumocystis carinii* pneumonia (PCP), in five young, previously healthy, gay men in Los Angeles. As the timeline at HIV.gov recalls:

> All the men had other unusual infections as well, indicating that their immune systems were not working; two had already died by the time the report was published. This edition of the MMWR marked the first official reporting of what was to become known as the AIDS epidemic.[5]

Not long after this stunning revelation, Jerry Farwell, an American far-right Christian leader, simply said, "AIDS is the wrath of God upon homosexuals."[6] His fellow American conservative Patrick Buchanan put it this way, "The poor homosexuals—they have declared war upon Nature, and now Nature is exacting an awful retribution."[7] They cited several scriptural references, including Leviticus 18:22, 20:13; 1 Corinthians 6:9; and 1 Timothy 1:9, to justify their condemnation of homosexuals. They also leaned into Romans 1:27, which says, "Men did shameful things with other men, and as a result of this sin, they suffered within themselves the penalty they deserved." Many American clergy, especially in the American conservative and Christian right movements, presented HIV/AIDS as a deserved punishment for the sexual transgressor, using biblical proof-texting to support their lack of compassion.

For many years, the broader church refused to deal with its homophobia because of theologies like this. When the virus came to the scene, very few religious leaders were willing to open the door for dialogue to discuss how to overcome its fears. Instead, those who were infected with the virus felt shut out of this community they so valued. The church has consistently failed to realize that people in their communities and congregations are affected by this virus. The epidemic even touches those in the ministry. Reverend Kwabena Rainey Cheeks, a pastor who has been HIV positive for fourteen years, says, "When you deal with AIDS you have to deal with all of the issues, all of the 'isms' of the community. . . . You can't touch AIDS and not deal with homophobia."[8]

To be honest, homosexuality and lesbianism did not arrive just when HIV/AIDS came onto the scene in 1981. The church allowed same-sex/gender-loving people to actively participate in leadership and other roles in the church. While some ministers would speak harshly against them during their sermons on Sunday, there were also ministers who were accepting of same-sex or same-gender-loving people. However, when the first case of AIDS began to claim the lives of many of their members, the wall of discrimination and stigmatization went up in the church. This wall of exclusion was erected in order to protect the reputation of the church and to ensure the church would not suffer any financial deficit due to having individuals who have a virus caused by committing sexual immorality.

GENDER, SEX, AND THE BIBLE

Another theological issue that affects the church's response to people living with HIV/AIDS is sex, a topic from which the church usually shies away. For the first ten to fifteen years of the HIV/AIDS epidemic, the primary victims were gay men, but the number of infected women, children, and senior adults has risen over time—because it is transmitted sexually and through reproduction. The church could respond to this development by holding a town hall meeting to discuss in great detail that individuals are sexual beings. They could discuss how Christian believers can accept themselves as sexual beings and how Christians can learn to control their sexual desires. Conversations about sex need to take place in our congregations. This type of dialogue can be held during a Wednesday night Bible study or even in small-group settings. A thorough understanding of how the Bible describes the purpose of sex will help facilitate greater knowledge, and it will help clarify how this one three-letter word has been abused and misused.

According to the scriptures, sex has two main purposes: procreation and pleasure. The doctrines of many mainline denominations hold that both purposes should fall under marriage. The following scriptures support these points: Genesis 1:27, Psalm 128:3, and Proverbs 5:15-19. Kelly Brown Douglas, a noted womanist theologian, makes the following statement related to how Christians should view sexuality:

> Human sexuality must be viewed as a gift from God. It is not, as spiritualistic dualism suggests, a human flaw. Rather it is significant to the human capacity to show forth the image of God. Sexuality allows human beings to be in loving relationships that are inevitably life-affirming and life-producing. Women and men must then know and experience who they are as children of God created in God's own image.[9]

When churches accept the fact that human sexuality is a gift and not a curse, then the churches can open up dialogue about sex and having safer sex. In a report released by Child Trends Data Bank, more than one-third of high school students reported being sexually active. In 2013, thirty-three percent of males in grades nine through twelve reported being sexually active, and thirty-five percent of females in grades nine through twelve reported being sexually active.[10] We can see from these statistics how important it is for teenagers to learn the true meaning and purpose of sex from the church—and not from peers, television shows, music videos, social media outlets, and other sources. What kinds of educational opportunities could your church offer?

The potential for positive change that can come from a church-based sex-ed program cannot be overstated. With proper education and teaching, the number of sexually transmitted diseases will decrease—especially the number of new HIV/AIDS infection cases. The impact of this virus can be reduced dramatically. Counselors Casey T. Tobin, Jenny Duncan, and Courtney Frank write, "What one believes about an issue will influence one's perception and experience with situations related to that issue. When individuals learn about sex, what one learns, what one's attitude toward sex and sexuality is, and the reflection of sexuality on one's behaviors all has personal and professional significance."[11] Shouldn't the churches have a role in this important aspect of personal formation?

Parents and caregivers might also find themselves in need of support from the church on this topic. After all, many households remain silent on the subject of sex. Many parents fail to have this deep discussion with their children until one of them becomes pregnant or gets someone pregnant. Dr. Phil, a noted television talk show host and licensed counselor, penned a book with John Chirban titled *How to Talk with Your Kids about Sex*. They suggest that parents and caregivers should begin to have this conversation at an early age, and this conversation should be ongoing. They say that kids begin to ask questions about their private parts and where babies come from as young as four and five years old. The book recommends that the adults in the family start the conversation when their kids ask the first question. They advise parents to call the parts by their medical terms and explain the purposes for these body parts.

Many homes lack specific knowledge about how and when to have these kinds of conversations. Oftentimes, parents want to wait until the kids reach the age of puberty. In many cases, kids have already experienced some form of sexual acts by this age. When this conversation is taking place, the talk needs to include a discussion of how sex was created by God and the dos and don'ts related to sex. Kids must feel comfortable enough with their parents to feel free to ask questions or share information about sex without the fear of being judged and punished. We need to break the generational cycle of parents not sharing this information, and the church can be part of this transformation. There are too many teenage pregnancies and kids testing positive for sexually transmitted diseases—including kids testing positive for HIV/AIDS.

WHY DOES THIS MATTER THEOLOGICALLY?

Many Christians understand the subject of sex through the biblical interpretation that sex was created by God for the purpose of procreation and pleasure between a man and a woman. Many who hold those beliefs label individuals who step outside of this original plan of sexual activity as fornicators, adulterators, and even prostitutes, based on their reading of 1 Corinthians 6:9-10.

In addition to leaning on this passage, some in the broader church also took on the attitude of pre-Christ teachings, which was to view these individuals as outcasts. To support this concept, they applied ideas from Leviticus chapters 13 and 14, which offer authoritative procedures for handling individuals who are suffering from a serious skin disease. The passage of scripture states that people with this disease must be presented to the priest to determine if the individual is ceremonially clean or unclean. If the individual is determined to be unclean, the individual must be quarantined for seven days. If the skin has not cleared up, then the individual must remain in quarantine for seven additional days. This practice was used in order to cause public judgment upon those individuals who were infected.

What a sad indictment of the church! Here it was the churches who were forbidding sick individuals from coming to the hospital in order to be healed. In the words of theologian Robin Gill, "Christian theology has, sometimes unintentionally, operated in such a way as to reinforce the stigma and to increase the likelihood of discrimination."[12] Would God be pleased with the action of the church? How would God address this subject matter with individuals on Judgment Day?

Gill defines the word *stigma* as "the branding or labeling of a person or a group of persons as being unworthy of inclusion in the human community, and it results in discrimination and ostracization."[13] African Americans know firsthand how discrimination and stigmatization can affect an individual's self-esteem. This practice reduces the self-value and self-worth of any individual. When people are on the receiving end of this practice, they have a greater risk of experiencing more health issues and begin to walk away from God. According to theologian Gillian Patterson:

> For theology, stigma is first and foremost an ethical issue: it is about truth; and it connects with our broad understanding of what it means to be a human being. AIDS-related stigmas also invite reflection from the sub-disciplines of ecclesiology, missiology, and public theology: it has implications for the Church as community or communities, its

> mission in the world, and its role in relation to the rest of civil society. It has implications for church history and for biblical studies in that it relates to the attitudes that stem from the tradition of the Church, and also to the way scriptures and other texts have been transmitted and interpreted. Stigma is also a Christological question, raising issues about incarnation, salvation, and about what it means for the Church to be "the Body of Christ."[14]

The question the church must answer is: Would Jesus approve or disapprove of the church's negative response? Has the church failed to be a place of refuge and hope for congregants who are marginalized, for those who are the least of these, lost and left out because of their health status? Individuals who are living with the virus are searching for an answer to these questions: "Does Christ still love me?" and "Will my status preclude me from entering into heaven?"

The Hope of Liberation Theology for those with HIV/AIDS

Mark 1:40-44 shares how a man with leprosy came to Jesus, requesting that he would heal him. Jesus showed compassion by touching him, and the man was cleansed from his leprosy. Jesus recognized the customs of the area and knew, based on the Levitical law, that if anybody touched someone with leprosy, they were considered to be unclean. Jesus disregarded the law, pushed past the stigma, and showed compassion. The man came to Jesus with a humble spirit and in need of healing. So, Jesus took the necessary steps to honor the request of the man.

In order to join Jesus in offering healing, the church should work to dispel the stigma associated with HIV/AIDS and end discrimination. Robin Gill reflects:

> The stigmatization of others is a sin far greater than most of the so-called "misdeeds" on which HIV infection is often

> blamed. After all, the sinful attitudes, most frequently identified by Jesus as being incompatible with his Kingdom, were pride, self-righteousness, exclusivity, hypocrisy and the misuse of power: all of them ingredients in the deadly cocktails that causes stigma.[15]

One of the ways to work for the healing and inclusion of people with the virus in the church is to change the rhetoric by offering a message of hope, encouraging people to release their fear and judgment as it relates to HIV/AIDS. Every day, people living with HIV/AIDS face the feeling of being alone, due to keeping their status secret from family members, close friends, and co-workers. These individuals are battling psychological and sociological issues associated with the virus. However, the theological battles they face are in answering these questions: Where is God in their current situation? Has God forsaken them? Does God still love them?

Individuals living with the virus desire to hear from the church that the promises of hope found in scripture still apply to them. One example can be found in Genesis 41:51-52, which says, "Joseph named his oldest son Manasseh, which means, God has made me to forget all of my troubles and everyone who is my father's family. Joseph named his second son Ephraim, for he said, 'God has made me fruitful in this land of my grief.'" A way of interpreting this scripture through a lens of hope might be to share a message to people living with HIV/AIDS that God will allow them to forget all their troubles and be fruitful in the land living with the virus. Other examples could be drawn from the Gospel according to Luke. In the eighteenth chapter, several parables can encourage the reader with two major points: instructions to pray always and never give up, and examples of who has faith.

A sermon based on this scripture could help encourage individuals who are living with the virus to never give up on life and on God. When a person has constant and consistent communication with Jesus Christ, he or she will not be alone—this message is true for all people. Jesus will protect, provide, and keep his promises to never forsake those who trust him. Instead of the spirit of judgment and condemnation, these kinds of sermonic expressions are needed to usher in the ministry of compassion. Clergy and church members must remember that people living with the virus are living with a good deal of self-condemnation on a daily basis and experiencing society's continuous lack of support.

James Cone, a noted Black Liberation Theologian, says, "When the oppressed are passive and afraid of the struggle of freedom, then they must be reminded that the gospel is identical with their liberation from political bondage."[16] Unfortunately, people living with HIV/AIDS feel oppressed by the virus first and foremost, then by society, and last but not least, by the church. Cone strongly expresses the view that "the task of theology is to show the significance of the oppressor's struggle against inhuman powers, relating the people's struggle to God's intention to set them free. Theologians must make the gospel clear in particular social context so that God's people will know that their struggle for freedom is God's struggle too."[17]

In the biblical narrative of Naaman, found in the fifth chapter of the Second book of Kings, we hear about how Naaman was one of the most respected and successful army generals, but he had leprosy. According to the Levitical Law, Naaman was supposed to be isolated from his family, soldiers, and society in general until he was deemed clean by the priest. At the urging of one of his servants, Naaman went to the king; however, the king felt the presence of Naaman was a set-up by the king's enemy. When Elisha heard of the situation, he requested for Naaman to come to him. When Naaman arrived at Elisha's house, instead of Elisha coming to the door, Elisha's servant or armor-bearer came and handed Naaman a message from Elisha. The message told Naaman to go and wash in the Jordan River seven times. After receiving the message from the armor-bearer, Naaman became angry.

Arguably, Naaman felt disappointed that the man of God did not come to the door to speak to him. Naaman believed that due to his health status, the prophet would not want to be associated with him and also did not want to be labeled unclean. Thousands of years later, many men and women of God failed to come to the door of the church to greet people living with HIV/AIDS.

History repeats itself. First, the church failed to speak out in support of justice for people of color during the period of slavery, Jim Crow, and other discriminatory practices. Then, for more than forty years, many churches refused to take a social and political stand in the fight to prevent the spread of HIV/AIDS. Due to the silence of the church on this serious pandemic issue, many parishioners sit in the pews, hiding their status because of the fear of experiencing discrimination. The church continues to provide a place of refuge for those individuals living with other conditions but fails to include in their altar call prayer requests to God to heal those people living with HIV/AIDS. Until the church takes the responsibility to follow Jesus' teaching as it relates to providing ministry of compassion and affirmation of God's love, it will continue to miss the mark and fail to truly receive the full blessings from God. Now is the time to be like Jesus by opening your arms and heart.

Reflection Questions

1. What actions can you take to offer hope to individuals who are living with a chronic illness?
2. How can scriptures be offered to comfort and encourage those who are living with the virus?
3. How can we break the historical cycle of discrimination and exclusion?
4. How can we share accurate knowledge of HIV/AIDS in order to dispel stigma?

NOTES

1. E. A. Hoffman, "I Must Tell Jesus" (1894). In the public domain, per https://hymnary.org/text/i_must_tell_jesus_all_of_my_trials.
2. "Theology," Merriam-Webster Dictionary, accessed April 21, 2014, http://www.merriam-webster.com/dictionary/theology.
3. Owen C. Thomas and Ellen K. Wondra, *Introduction to Theology* (New York: Morehouse Publishing, 2002), 1.
4. Edward L. Smith, *The Doctrines of Providence and Revelation: An Introduction to Philosophy and Theology: A Series in Postmodern Studies*, vol. 6 (Atlanta: The Research Center Press, 2001), 50.
5. "A Timeline of AIDS," AIDS, 27 March 2014, https://www.hiv.gov/hiv-basics/overview/history/hiv-and-aids-timeline#year-1981, accessed October 1, 2024.
6. Matt Stearns, "Jerry Falwell: 1933–2007," *McClatchy Newspapers*, March 27, 2014, http://www.dailypress.com, accessed October 1, 2024.
7. "Sin, Sex and Science: The HIV/AIDS Crisis," Michigan State University, accessed March 27, 2014, http://www.history.msu.edu/hst425/resources/online-essays/sin-sex-and-science-the-hivaids-crisis, accessed October 1, 2024.
8. Kelly Brown Douglas, *Sexuality and the Black Church: A Womanist Perspective* (Maryknoll, NY: Orbis Books, 2008), 3.
9. Douglas, *Sexuality and the Black Church*, 121.
10. Child Trends, "Sexual Activity Among Teens," DataBank, accessed May 14, 2014, https://www.childtrends.org/indicators/sexual-activity-among-teens.
11. Casey T. Tobin, Jenny Duncan, and Courtney Frank, "Sexuality: Are We Practicing What We Are Preaching," Counseling, accessed October 5, 2013, http://www.counseling.org/articles-are-we-practicing-what-we-are-preaching.
12. Robin Gill, *Reflecting Theologically on AIDS: A Global Challenge* (London: SCM Press, 2007), 19.
13. Gill, *Reflecting Theologically on AIDS: A Global Challenge* (London: SCM Press, 2007), 19.
14. Gillian Patterson, *AIDS Related Stigma: Thinking Outside of the Box: The Theological Challenge* (Geneva, Switzerland: Ecumenical Advocacy Alliance and the World Council of Churches, 2005), 6.
15. Gill, *Reflecting Theologically on AIDS: A Global Challenge* (London: SCM Press, 2007), 20.
16. James H. Cone, *God of the Oppressed* (Maryknoll, NY: Orbis Books, 1997), 89.
17. Cone, *God of the Oppressed,* (Maryknoll, NY: Orbis Books, 1997), 90–91.

CHAPTER FIVE

HISTORY REPEATS ITSELF

IN 2017, A woman entered a dental office in a major city for a tooth cleaning. "Do you have any major health concerns that would help the dentist in caring for your needs?" the receptionist asked. The woman quietly replied, hoping that the others in the waiting room would not hear her, "Yes, I am HIV positive."

The receptionist, with a panicked look on her face, stood up quickly and went to another room. When she returned, the office manager was with her. "The receptionist told me about your condition," the office manager began. "Unfortunately, we are not equipped to handle your needs in this office, so it is our policy not to treat patients with HIV or AIDS. We cannot serve you here for the safety of the doctors and staff."

Embarrassed and angry, the woman left the office. "What am I to do?" she prayed. "How am I supposed to take care of my dental health if nobody will treat me, even for a simple tooth cleaning?"

The next day, she went to a law firm to see if it was legal for a dental office to deny patient services due to health status. The lawyers eagerly took the case. They went to a bench trial several years later, where the judge ruled in favor of the woman, who was financially awarded for her experience of discrimination. "Hopefully my experience can help others avoid the embarrassment and hassle I've endured," she reflected. "The money helps, but what makes me feel better is that others have their right to equal care protected."

What the woman experienced in the dental office was very unfortunate. There must be a change of culture in the attitudes of individuals who are living with HIV/AIDS. Continuing this type of negativity will expand the cycle of discrimination, inclusion, and separation for years to come. The founding fathers of this country envisioned that all citizens would be treated equally regardless of their gender, sexual orientation, race, and even health conditions. The responsibility rests upon our shoulders to make a change.

The Fabric of a Culture

The thread of discrimination seems to have been deeply woven into the history of the United States. We can easily identify three major periods in the history of the United States where this is apparent, such as slavery, Jim Crow, and the Civil Rights Movement. From the time when the first slave ship arrived in Jamestown, the deplorable treatment of African-descended people began. This division of racial and ethnic groups had negative effects on the economic, educational, financial, and even spiritual aspects of this group of people. This vicious cycle of inhumane treatment continues to be passed down from generation to generation as learned behavior, as each new generation continues a practice of discrimination, instilling a spirit of racial hatred against others because of the color of their skin.

Discrimination is not limited to the workplace, restaurants, and healthcare facilities, but this practice can be found in churches, mosques, and synagogues. It is even found in the Bible. One of the first documented instances of discrimination is found in the Hebrew Bible when Moses' family members were disappointed with his marriage to an Ethiopian woman. Numbers 12:1-2 says, "While they were at Hazeroth, Miriam and Aaron criticized Moses because he had married a Cushite woman." In the New Testament, Jesus referred to a cultural norm in which Jews did not communicate with other ethnic groups when he was speaking with the woman at the well. John 4:7-9 reads, "Soon a Samaritan woman came to draw water, and Jesus said to her, 'Please give me a drink.' He was alone at the time because his disciples had gone into the village to buy some food. The woman was surprised, for Jews refuse to have anything to do with Samaritans." The sad indictment is that the practice of discrimination is now observed in congregations to those congregants living with HIV/AIDS.

Prior to January 1, 1863 (when African Americans received their freedom from slavery), several generations of African Americans had to endure the harsh task of working without being properly rewarded. During those years of slavery, church leaders endorsed the oppression and mistreatment of African Americans. These believers in God would use scriptural references as the foundation and justification of their treatment of enslaved people. For example, Ephesians 6:5-6 says, "Slaves, obey your earthly masters with deep respect and fear. Serve them sincerely as you would serve Christ. Try to please them all the time, not just when they are watching you." Also, Colossians 3:22 says, "Slaves obey your earthly masters in everything you do. Try to please them all the time, not just when they are watching you. Serve them sincerely because of your reverent fear of the Lord."

During the period of 1700–1799, there was a major push to educate slaves: with the passage of legislation, "Religion with Letters," many slave owners were permitted to teach their slaves to read and write. The Bible was one of the main reading materials used by slaves. In the book *Hell Without Fire*, professor of church history Love Henry Whelchel shares that many "slaveholders were skeptical of religious training for their slaves, fearing that training would make their slaves proud slaves."[1]

Many slaveholders held the religious community responsible for the slave revolts in the Southern states. Southern slaveholders believed that religious training gave slaves the opportunity to think for themselves and feel a sense of empowerment. In 1829, many Southern states passed legislation to prohibit teaching slaves how to read and write. After the passage of these laws in the Southern states, many missionaries and evangelists approved the plan for the oral religious training of slaves, training which one scholar termed "religion without letters."[2] Fredrick K. C. Price, founder and pastor of the Crenshaw Christian Center in Los Angeles, reflects on the church's history of complicity with discrimination saying, "We are giving the world a bad example because there is so much prejudice in the Church. That is why racism can exist in society the way it does. It all started when the preachers got into league with the slave owners, and the Church sanctioned slavery."[3]

On January 1, 1863, when African Americans received their freedom from slavery, many African Americans believed they had been granted freedom. After enduring more than 246 years of slavery and living under the oppression of white slave owners, this Emancipation Day was to be the start of a new beginning. Between the 1880s and the 1960s, many American states enforced segregation through the Jim Crow laws (named after a Black character in minstrel shows). Legal punishments were imposed on people for consorting with members of another race, especially by forbidding interracial marriages and ordering business owners and public institutions to keep their Black and white clientele separated.[4]

The Civil Rights Movement brought an end to the Jim Crow era in the United States. The movement exposed the American public to how discrimination practices toward people of color were not in agreement with the Constitution of the United States. A court ruling and legislation made it possible for people of color to obtain the freedom and opportunity to live out the meaning of the preamble of the Constitution, which declares that all men are created equal and have the right to pursue happiness. After the passage of several Civil Rights Acts and the ruling of the *Brown v. Topeka Board of Education* of 1954, people of color gained access to prestigious colleges, corporate offices, major sporting teams, and more. Although the movement did not eliminate discrimination practices, the new policies hold individuals, companies, and organizations responsible for providing equal access to all Americans regardless of age, sex, gender, color, religious affiliation, or ethnic background.

Every year, local, state, and national governments pass legislation intended to reverse many of the civil rights actions. The reversal of civil rights actions is a sign that discrimination practices are still alive and widespread in American culture. As the practice continues to have life, many African American churches have remained silent and failed to become vocal on the dismantling of the Civil Rights Acts and affirmative action programs. In my eyes, the church remaining silent about the important subject matter of these unfair practices sends the signal that the African American churches endorse the practices of discrimination. It reminds me of what the humorist and writer Mark Twain reportedly once said, "History doesn't repeat itself, but it rhymes."

History Rhymes

In 1981, when the first case of HIV/AIDS became public, the culture intensified discriminating against another group of people: the gay community. At first, the virus affected members of the gay community in alarming proportions. This resulted in the American Red Cross enacting a policy that prohibited gay men from donating any blood out of fear of them passing on the virus. In 1991, Earvin "Magic" Johnson, the well-known professional basketball player, announced his early retirement from the NBA due to being diagnosed as HIV-positive—the league was concerned about possible transmission if he were to be injured on the court. Between the years of 1981 and 2021, any US Navy personnel who tested positive for the virus were removed immediately from their assigned ship duty station and reassigned to land (shore) duty. These individuals were banned from being assigned to any sea duty for the remainder of their naval career. In 2022, a court ruling ended the ban on people living with HIV joining the military. Discrimination against people with HIV/AIDS was a widely accepted cultural norm for a long time.

Once again, the church took part in playing a central role in how being HIV-positive became stigmatized. The stigma associated with this virus quickly reminded many Christian believers of the treatment of individuals who were affected with leprosy in biblical times. These affected individuals were isolated from their families, friends, co-workers, and society in general, and they remained in isolation until the priest was able to declare them clean.

There are many stories of churches refusing to hold funeral services or memorial services for individuals whose death was classified as AIDS-related due to people believing that the deceased must have had a same-sex lifestyle. Even with the latest research and progress related to the treatment of HIV/AIDS, many churches continue this practice in the twenty-first century. Once again, the church has a golden opportunity to curtail the practice of discrimination, but too many churches remain silent. The discriminatory practice continues every Wednesday or Tuesday evening during Bible study when a pastor refuses to have a dialogue on the HIV/AIDS subject. The bigoted practice continues every Sunday morning, as prayers for healing are being offered up for those parishioners who are battling other diseases but not for those living with the virus that causes AIDS.

Some progress has been made in the fight to combat the spread of disease with more churches having established HIV/AIDS ministries, which help educate and offer other services to the community. In the words of AME presiding elder C. Dennis Williams, "HIV/AIDS is not just a problem for the local church; it is a global problem that has the capacity to destroy the very essence of life."[5]

For more than four hundred years, the practice of discrimination has been a thorn in our society. The hatred directed at a specific group of people due to the color of their skin, sexual orientation, gender, education level, and now because of their health conditions goes against the teaching of loving your neighbor as yourselves. Most individuals see the church as a refuge or haven of solace and God's presence for comfort, strength, and healing. However, we plainly see how the church has endorsed this form of separation and oppression. The silent voice of church leaders during challenging times was a tacit sign of acceptance and not a condemnation of this biased practice against the children of God. God made the following statement: "If someone says, 'I love God,' but hates a fellow believer, that person is a liar, for if we don't love people we can see, how can we love God, whom we cannot see?" (1 John 4:20, NLT). Those in the church who do not show compassion to their fellow believers have perjured themselves. The evidence demonstrates that they express hate toward individuals because of their color, education level, gender, sexual orientation, and health conditions.

Many churches refuse to offer HIV/AIDS education to prevent the virus from spreading in their communities, even though many of their houses of worship are located in neighborhoods with high HIV/AIDS infection rates. What will it take for the church to realize that HIV/AIDS affects all? Nobody is immune to potential infection by this virus. Through modern medicine and continuous research projects, the virus is no longer seen as a death sentence, simply considered a chronic illness. However, the stigma that comes with the virus is still negative. Medical anthropologist Jean Scandlyn wrote in the *Western Journal of Medicine*, "On the national level, AIDS as a chronic illness means a shift in the priority it receives in national health policy and a growing inequity in how resources for its treatment are allocated among the population."[6]

What's Next?

Churches and members of the religious community must remember that their voices have power and can influence the world when they speak up about injustice. Now is the time for the church to open a dialogue amongst the congregation on how to get rid of discrimination. Once the dialogue begins in the houses of worship, it will spill over into the community, city councils, state legislatures, and members of Congress. Individuals should not be treated differently because of the color of their skin, age, gender, sexual orientation, or religious beliefs, and most importantly, people should not be treated differently because they are living with HIV/AIDS or any other health condition.

To begin a conversation about dispelling the stigma of HIV/AIDS in the church, you could host a town hall meeting with a panel consisting of individuals who are living with the virus and medical professionals. During this panel discussion, allow those individuals to share with the audience the highs and lows of living daily life with a virus that many people still incorrectly classify as a homosexual disease. Seek panel members who have been living with the virus for at least five years or longer. Each of their stories will be different, but the stories will be very impactful to the audience. The medical professionals on the panel will be able to share more educational information on how research and treatment have progressed in the last ten to twenty years. During the town hall meeting, members who are living with the virus could share with the congregation how they can provide spiritual care and the affirmation of God's love toward them.

Another opportunity for churches to dispel the stigma is by hosting services of remembrance for those who have died, as well as services honoring those individuals who are living with the virus. During these services, family members would be able to submit information about their loved ones who have succumbed to the virus and honor those individuals who are living productive lives. Another idea for these services is to recognize an individual, organization, or social service agency that works in the prevention and offering treatment to individuals who are living with the virus. Remember, the goal of the church is to offer hope and healing to all who seek the living water, and activities such as these can help ensure that individuals living with the virus can come to the well.

Reflection Questions

1. Have you ever witnessed someone being discriminated against because of their health status?
2. How would you feel if someone refused to sit next to you in church because of weight, clothing style, hair design, or some other feature of your personhood?
3. Have you ever assumed something about someone and was wrong? Did you ever apologize to the individual? Or has someone assumed something about you and was not accurate? How did these situations feel?
4. How can we, as congregation members, take the necessary steps to prevent the history of discrimination from repeating itself?

Notes

1. Love Henry Whelchel Jr., *Hell Without Fire* (Nashville: Abingdon Press, 2002), 49–50.
2. Whelchel Jr., *Hell Without Letters*, (Nashville: Abingdon Press, 2002), 65–66.
3. Frederick K. C. Price, *Race, Religion and Racism* (Los Angeles: Faith One Publishing, 1999), 14–15.
4. "Jim Crow Laws," National Park Service, accessed February 21, 2014, http://www.nps.gov/malu/forteachers/jim_crow_laws.htm, accessed October 1, 2024.

5. C. Dennis Williams, *An Ecclesiastical Model for HIV/AIDS Ministry* (Bloomington, IN: Author House, 2010), xi.
6. Jean Scandlyn, "When AIDS Became A Chronic Illness," *Western Journal of Medicine* 172, no. 2 (February 2000): 130–133, accessed September 13, 2013, http://www.ncbi.nlm.nih.gov/pmc/articles/pmc1070775, accessed 1 October 2024.

CHAPTER SIX

A LOOK INSIDE AND OUTSIDE THE CHURCH WALLS

Romans 12:2 urges us to "be not conformed to this world be transformed by renewing our minds." Like when the children of Israel chose a king to rule over them, religion has often been heavily influenced by culture. Culture has been dictated by mostly non-religious people or people who use religious language only for their personal gains. In modern times, the church and society find themselves in major arguments that put the woke-minded against the anti-woke-minded, diversity against cultural uniformity. Sadly, much of the religious community is taking their cue from culture rather than leading based on the teachings of Jesus Christ. Unfortunately, when it comes to expressing compassion to those who are living with HIV/AIDS, the broader culture is currently meeting the needs more than much of the church. When will the church take back its rightful place as the trendsetter and lead the path forward?

How do other congregations and disciplines provide compassion and ministry to those individuals who are living with the virus? Are there positive examples from which we in the church can learn? As we consider these questions, we will examine the historical, biblical, and theological approaches of these ministries and disciplines in the United States and in Africa.

Positive Examples for Ministry Practice

Almost all communities have churches, and churches are often valued as trusted sources of information and guidance. In many historical examples, churches' actions have been a catalyst for positive social changes (e.g., abolition, civil rights). Churches deliver a wide range of services to their congregants and surrounding communities. These services include direct delivery of counseling and transportation as well as information related to employment, housing, finances, and health care. While churches are clearly important social services providers, many churches have also operated in ways that have stigmatized a variety of conditions, either through their overt condemnation of groups and behaviors or through ignoring important issues. As we read earlier, many churches initially responded to HIV by attributing it to homosexuality and social decay. However, many churches have provided a variety of HIV/AIDS-related services over the last two decades. At the same time, some churches have still limited their involvement in HIV prevention and care because of archaic moral codes and beliefs about sin.[1]

Dennis Williams formed Grace Ministries as the project during his tenure as senior pastor of Bethel African Methodist Episcopal Church in San Diego, California. This ministry has been in operation for eleven years. This ministry serves as a non-judgmental, confidential, discreet, and compassionately spiritual hope-filled place. It is an action place where people are important and valued. This ministry provides vital links between care facilities, private and public social services, and HIV/AIDS programs nationally, statewide, and locally. They provide young people with HIV/AIDS education and encourage them to maintain a responsible sexual attitude regarding STDs, recreational drug use, and alcohol through its Safe Youth Program. Grace Ministries provides a safe place where myths, misinformation, and other issues related to HIV/AIDS are discussed openly while being responsive to the sensitivities of the church, including all forms of transmissions, prevention, and safe practices. Grace Ministries also offers housing through Richard Place, which provides apartments for individuals with HIV/AIDS. Residents of Richard Place receive individual counseling, peer-to-peer counseling, and a mealtime program, in addition to a place to live.[2]

Another notable HIV/AIDS ministry from an evangelical perspective is at Saddleback Church in California, where Rick and Kay Warren served as pastors. They have a strong HIV/AIDS initiative, and they encourage other churches to participate in the fight to curtail this pandemic. They use the letters of the word *church* as an acronym to represent six steps in which a church can engage in prevention, treatment, care, and support:

C – Care for and Support the Sick. The care component includes offering training on HIV 101 and other latest resources concerning the virus. Start a support group for those who are living with the virus and finally create a CARE Team, which would serve as a one-on-one buddy person to those who are living with the virus.

H – Handle HIV Testing and Counseling. Provide HIV testing to the congregation and community at large.

U – Unleash a Volunteer Force. Build a volunteer force willing to help minister to the needs and concerns of people living with the virus.

R – Remove the Stigma and associated discrimination that is associated with the virus. An individual who is living with the virus should never be asked how they became infected with the disease. But how can we help you?

C – Champion Healthy Behavior by educating on healthy sexual behavior with an emphasis on spiritual abstinence. Also, provide information about how they can live a drug-free life.

H – Help with HIV Medication Distribution by offering pre-treatment preparation, treatment education, and adherence support for the entire family.[3]

The Allen Temple Baptist Church AIDS Ministry of Oakland, California, a faith-based organization, seeks to combat the fear, prejudice, and lack of knowledge that surrounds HIV/AIDS by providing critical medical and social services, as well as prevention awareness education. The ministry was established in 1987. They offer the following programs:

- Prevention awareness education
- Prayer and spiritual guidance
- Medical treatment and life-saving HIV/AIDS antiretroviral medication
- Living and social services

The ministry focuses on overall solutions to reduce the trends of higher infection rates amongst African Americans and Sub-Saharan Africans, increase awareness and combat HIV/AIDS stigmatism, sustain the lives of people living with HIV/AIDS, and expand the reach of services through leadership development opportunities. To that end, they actively encourage other churches to create HIV/AIDS ministries. Their efforts focus deeply and solely on two geographic areas of the world presently in crisis: East Oakland, California, and Zimbabwe, Africa. In East Oakland and surrounding communities, the ministry provides HIV/AIDS medical and social services and prevention awareness education to people at risk, especially high-risk youth and young adults. In Zimbabwe, they provide HIV/AIDS medical treatment, life-saving HIV/AIDS antiretroviral medication, and prevention awareness education to Africans in grave need, as well as essential living support to orphaned children.[4]

The biblical lesson that resonates with the Allen Temple ministry is where Jesus speaks on the Final Judgment, stating that the way people should treat others (even "the least of these") will be the criterion of judgment. What if other churches followed this lead? How could your church implement some of these ministries to positively impact your community?

Positive Examples from Denominational Bodies and National Organizations

What are churches doing at the denominational level to address the issue of discrimination and remove the stigma associated with HIV/AIDS? In 2014, I examined the main websites of the National Baptist Convention, USA; the Progressive National Baptist Convention; the Presbyterian Church, USA; the Church of God in Christ; and the United Church of Christ, hoping to find official statements on how they are addressing the HIV/AIDS epidemic. Unfortunately, none of these denominations had developed a plan of action or had not posted a statement on their websites at that time. But this does not mean that no work is happening at the national or denominational levels.

During their 219th General Assembly in 2010, the Presbyterian Church, USA, adopted a report titled "Becoming an HIV and AIDS Competent Church: Prophetic Witness and Compassionate." In the report, the denomination's Advisory Committee on Social Witness Policy addressed the HIV/AIDS pandemic in the United States and globally. The report addressed the issue of how the denomination had played a role in offering compassion and being the voice of support from the onset of the disease. However, the PCUSA denomination recognizes the need to be more compassionate as an organization and also encourages local churches to become more active in the fight to curtail this pandemic.

The PCUSA committee recommends that the denomination participate in a program known as the HIV-competent church program. The HIV-competent church was created by the World Council of Churches (WCC). HIV-competent churches are called to develop institutional and theological capacity in a socially relevant, inclusive, sustainable, and collaborative way that reduces the spread of HIV, improves the lives of the infected and affected, mitigates the impact of HIV, and ultimately restores.[5] The program is similar to other HIV/AIDS ministry programs that provide education, medication distribution, and prevention. The report mentioned providing a safe place for people who are living with the virus; however, the content fails to address key theological questions that are typical concerns of people living with the virus (Is God still present in my life? Does God still love me? Has God abandoned me? Will my illness preclude me from inheriting the Kingdom of God?).

Other national organizations are fighting for the cause of eliminating the spread of this disease. These organizations also are pushing for local, state, and federal legislation and offering programs for communities of faith and other social services that work closely with individuals who are living with HIV/AIDS. One African American National organization is the National Black Leadership Commission on AIDS, Inc. (NBLCA), which is described as "The oldest and largest non-profit organization of its kind in the United States." NBLCA's key activities include capacity-building training, technical assistance, education, policy advocacy, screening, testing, referrals, research, evaluation, resource development, and leadership development.[6]

Another organization is The Balm In Gilead, Inc., known throughout Africa and the United States for its insightful understanding of religious cultures and values and extraordinary ability to build strong, trusted partnerships with faith communities.[7] One of The Balm In Gilead's major initiatives is the African American Denominational Leadership Health Initiative (AADLHI). In March 2005, they launched AADLHI in partnership with the National Women's Missionary Societies of the African Methodist Episcopal Church (AME), the African

Methodist Episcopal Zion Church (AME Zion), and the Christian Methodist Episcopal Church (CME). The Balm In Gilead's decision to engage the national leadership of the women's missionary societies was determined by the thinking and knowledge that African American women are at high risk for HIV/AIDS, cervical cancer, and far too many other health concerns. The three historical Black Methodist denominations were chosen because of their long-standing commitment to social change through education, social justice, and determination.

The Women's Missionary Societies of these three Methodist denominations have historically anchored the Christian movement for over four centuries within the United States and abroad. This partnership represents the first time that African American church denominations have joined with a non-governmental organization to strengthen their internal organizational structures for the purpose of engaging the denomination at every level in the provision of health education, service, and compassionate support. The Balm In Gilead provides ongoing training and technical support in the appointment and capacity development of health coordinators at every level of church governance to ensure the full engagement and provision of quality health education and disease prevention interventions for everyone.

The AADLHI seeks to develop and implement a sustainable health education and service delivery system within each denomination to address the challenges of HIV/AIDS, cervical cancer, and other health disparities disproportionately affecting African Americans. The main objectives of this initiative are:

1. Enhance and strengthen the capacity of each denomination to establish an Office of Health within the national headquarters of the national women's missionary society that will support the full engagement of the church at all levels of governance, including the local church.

2. Enhance and strengthen the capacity of each Episcopal district of the AME, AME Zion, and CME denominations to support the engagement of local churches in developing an effective and appropriate response to HIV/AIDS, cervical cancer, and other health disparities within their congregations and communities.
3. Provide training and technical support to the leadership of the national missionary societies that will strengthen their capacity to provide and coordinate strategic planning, training, implementation, and evaluation of health education and service interventions at the Episcopal and presiding elder district levels and throughout the entire denominational membership.
4. Provide training and technical support at the Episcopal and presiding elder district levels that will empower and support the ability of the leadership and laity to effectively engage and implement health service delivery interventions at the local church and community level.[8]

WHAT CAN WE LEARN FROM THESE EXAMPLES?

In the forty-plus years that the church has been wandering in the wilderness, unsure of how to appropriately address the needs of individuals and the community in the HIV/AIDS epidemic, we have seen positive and negative examples of ministries. According to the World Health Organization (WHO), an estimated more than thirty-nine million have died since the first cases were reported in 1981, and 1.3 million have died since of AIDS-related cases in 2022.[9] The church has some bright spots in addressing this pandemic that has no respect of persons, regardless of age, gender, and ethnicity. The same WHO report states that approximately thirty-five million people worldwide are living with the virus. Some of these individuals may have reached the comfort level of sharing their status with family, friends, and church members. However, many of these individuals may still be afraid to share their status out of fear of being stigmatized and experiencing discrimination.

Although some non-profit organizations have taken responsibility for providing resources and programs to communities to fight this war, these organizations cannot and should not do this alone. From the beginning of time, the church has been a catalyst and leading force in offering social services and being the epicenter of meeting the community's needs. The needs of people living with the virus exceed the spiritual and include—but are not limited to—education, political advocacy, social justice, financial resources, and psychological well-being. Sadly, the church has collectively failed to include overt teaching about how to dispel stigma or end discrimination against people who are living with the virus in our Christian education curricula. Until we address these judgmental practices, the church will continue to lose credibility.

We have been given several blueprints of how to provide a holistic approach to ministry to individuals who are living with HIV/AIDS through the ministries of Allen Temple Baptist Church, The Balm In Gilead, and Saddlebrook Church. These ministries provide us with various methods of addressing the number of concerns related to this sensitive topic, including how the church can dispel the stigma associated with HIV/AIDS. Each of these programs was contextually designed for a specific population in their community and congregation. It is through these experiences the scripture texts of Isaiah 61:1-3 and Luke 4:18-19 come to life and individuals who are receiving this awesome work are being healed, edified, and affirmed spiritually. Individuals are being uplifted physically and emotionally. Finally, these types of ministries demonstrate how the church works outside of the walls of a brick-and-mortar building to offer services to a community of people who have been marginalized because of their positive diagnosis of a virus.

Reflection Questions

1. Which of the organization's programs could be instituted at your congregation?
2. What are your initial thoughts on the program at Saddlebrook Church?
3. If you tested positive for HIV/AIDS, who would be the first person you would share?
4. If you were diagnosed with HIV/AIDS with one of these programs, would you feel comfortable participating?

Notes

1. Shayna Cunningham et al., "The Role of Structure Versus Individual Agency in Churches' Responses to HIV/AIDS: A Case Study of Baltimore City Churches," *Journal of Religion and Health* 50, no. 2 (June 2011): 408–409.
2. C. Dennis Williams, *An Ecclesiastical Model for HIV/AIDS Ministry* (Bloomington, IN: Author House, 2010), 49.
3. Kay Warren, "HIV/AIDS Initiative Saddleback Church: What Every Church can do for People Living with HIV and AIDS," Kay Warren, accessed May 21, 2015, http://kaywarren.com/hiv.
4. "Allen Temple Baptist Church AIDS Ministry," Allen Temple, http://www.allen-temple.org, accessed May 21, 2015.
5. "United in Battling HIV/AIDS: A Guide to Understanding How Faith Communities Can Make a Difference," National Alliance of State and Territorial AIDS Directors, http://www.nastad.org/, accessed May 21, 2015.
6. "Mission of The National Black Leadership Commission on AIDS, Inc.," National Black Leadership Commission on AIDS, Inc., http://www.nblca.org/learn-about-nblca-2/mission/, accessed April 15, 2015.
7. "Mission of The Balm In Gilead," The Balm In Gilead, http://www.balmingilead.org/index.php/about/about-the-balm.html, accessed March 13, 2015.
8. "Objective of The Balm In Gilead," The Balm In Gilead, http://www.balmingilead.org/index.php/health-disparities-sub/health-disparities-initiatives/african-american-denominational-leadership-health-initiative/goals-a-objectives.html, accessed March 13, 2015.
9. "Global HIV/AIDS Overview," AIDS.gov, http://www.aids.gov/federal-resources/around-the-world/global-aids-overview/, accessed May 5, 2015.

CHAPTER SEVEN

WONDERFUL WORDS OF LIFE

When you are down in life or feeling desperate for a healing touch, where or to whom do you turn? Many people might say this to their friends and family. Others might say their pastors. But those of us who are Christians know that we can always rely on the Word of God to help us find and sustain hope in trying times. When life has you in the midst of a thunderstorm, feels like an earthquake, or tossing you like a tornado, how do you withstand those turbulent times? What procedure or emergency plan do you activate to bring peace and calm?

Basic Instructions for Life

The Bible contains basic instructions for life. We find various stories and situations that speak to our current situations—encouraging, enlightening, and challenging us to continue onward in life's journey. The same book may also provide corrective measures to be applied when individuals disobey any of the commandments or instructions. Sadly, this book also has a long history of being used by some people to enforce the separation of ethnic groups. For example, slave owners used the Bible to justify their inhumane treatment of enslaved people. We have also heard instances of how verses of the Bible have been used to justify the exclusion of people living with HIV/AIDS from full life in the church.

In ancient times, the Mosaic Laws were the primary legal guide, and remedies found in scripture were used when people were found guilty of breaking these laws. Holy Scriptures guided the moral trends of ancient society. For example, based on the Mosaic Laws found in the Hebrew Bible book of Leviticus, chapter 18, any sexual act that prohibited the process of procreation was considered an abomination. Thousands of years later, some people elect to use the same Leviticus to condemn people living with HIV/AIDS.

If the Bible is to be used as a moral guideline for society today, then why would certain passages be used to honor certain sins while condemning other sins? Genesis 1 and 2 indicate that God designed the earth to be paradise. However, from Genesis 3 to Revelation 20, paradise had been destroyed. Thus, the mission and goal of our engaging in the scripture text is to restore paradise to its origins. How can scripture be used in life-giving ways rather than as a tool for condemnation?

WORDS OF RESTORATION

Revelation 21 and 22 describe the restoration of paradise to its original design. Due to sin amongst the people of God, somebody had to pay the ransom on behalf of the children of God, so Jesus Christ came onto the scene. Jesus Christ's purpose was to redeem all people (Jews and Gentiles) from the penalty of sin and fulfill the prophecy of the prophets and teachers, allowing the children of God to have life and have it more abundantly. Jesus accomplished this daunting task by suffering the hardest punishment of humankind: death by crucifixion. The excellent news for all humankind is that Jesus rose from the dead, returned to sit at the right hand of God, and will return to claim his bride during the second coming. In the New Testament is found the mandate of loving one another as instituted by Jesus Christ. So, if this is the mandate for individuals who profess to be followers of Jesus

Christ, why do his followers so often fail to express love to all humankind?

The church is charged with ministering to the physical, emotional, and spiritual needs of its parishioners. Every church member should be afforded equal opportunity to receive emotional support, love, and comfort when needed. Each leader and member must recognize that the church's diverse makeup requires diverse methods for meeting the needs of each congregant. The twenty-first-century church needs to consider whether it is applying the biblical text as the standard operating procedure in meeting the members' needs.

When a member receives a serious diagnosis like HIV/AIDS, this is the time when these individuals need their church family to provide comfort and spiritual and emotional support. So, they come to the church house on a weekly basis in search of comfort and encouragement, but many times, they leave the church hurt, angry, and disappointed. These individuals often feel hurt due to the lack of compassion from the contents of the worship services. Why is the twenty-first-century church still practicing selective ministry for one congregational group while practicing oppressive ministry for another congregational group?

What Does the Bible Really Say?

Let's take a more in-depth look at two Hebrew Bible and two New Testament texts. We will use these to lay the foundation for providing a positive response to people who are living with HIV/AIDS. Isaiah 61:1 says, "The Spirit of the Sovereign Lord is upon me, for the Lord has anointed me to bring good news to the poor. He has sent me to comfort the brokenhearted and to proclaim that captives will be released and prisoners will be freed." Psalm 146:8b says, "The Lord lifts up those who are weighed down." We will take a deeper exegetical look at these passages of scriptures later in this chapter, focusing on the word of *comfort*.

Matthew 25:40 says, "And the King will say, 'I tell you the truth, when you did it to the one of the least of these my brothers and sisters, you were doing it to me!'" 1 Corinthians 15:54-58 says:

> Then, when our dying bodies have been transformed into bodies that will never die, the Scripture will be fulfilled: Death is swallowed up in victory. O death where is your victory? O death where is your sting? For sin is the sting that results in death, and the law gives sin its power. But thank God! He gives us victory over sin and death through our Lord Jesus Christ. So, my dear brothers and sisters are strong and immovable. Always work enthusiastically for the Lord, for you know that nothing you do for the Lord is ever useless.

I want to call your attention to the words *the least of these* and *victory* throughout these readings.

These foundational biblical texts resonate regarding offering ministry to the least of these. This includes those congregants living with HIV/AIDS. Throughout this book, we have established their need for comfort and our collective responsibility for informing them of their victory, which is in Christ Jesus, who is their Lord.

COMFORT MY PEOPLE

The prophet Isaiah provides a message to the people of Israel as they are released once again from the hands of their enemies: "The Spirit of the Sovereign Lord is upon me for he has anointed me to preach the good news to the poor. He has sent me to comfort the brokenhearted and to proclaim that captives will be released and prisoners will be freed" (Isaiah 61:1). Isaiah recognizes the hurt and pain of his people, and it is in this verse that the prophet changes his role. For many years, he instructed the people to repent and return to the supreme God, but with these words the prophet takes on the role of a counselor.

Merriam-Webster defines the word *comfort* as giving strength and hope to console, consolation, and freedom from pain and trouble.[1] The word *comfort* can be found seventy-nine times in seventy-two verses in the New Living Translations. The first mention of comfort to the children of Israel is found in Isaiah 40:1, "'Comfort, comfort my people,' says your God. 'Speak tenderly to Jerusalem. Tell her that her sad days are gone and her sins are pardoned. Yes, the Lord has punished her twice over for all of her sins.'" Other scriptures in the Old Testament pericope address the word *comfort*, Isaiah 66:12-13 says:

> This is what the Lord says: I will give Jerusalem a river of peace and prosperity. The wealth of the nations will flow to her. Her children will be nursed at her breasts, carried in her arms, and held on her lap. I will comfort you there in Jerusalem as a mother comforts her child.

Jeremiah 31:13 says, "The young women will dance for you, and the men- old and young—will join in the celebration. I will turn their mourning into joy. I will comfort them and exchange their sorrow for rejoicing." Lamentations 1:17 says, "Jerusalem reaches out for help but no one comforts her. Regarding his people Israel, the Lord has said, let their neighbors be their enemies! Let them be thrown away like a filthy rag!" Lamentations 1:21 says, "Others heard my groans, but no one turned to comfort me. When my enemies heard about my troubles, they were happy to see what you had done. Oh, bring the day you promised, when they will suffer as I have suffered." Zechariah 1:17 reads: "Say this also: This is what the LORD of Heaven's Armies say; the towns of Israel will again overflow with prosperity and the Lord will again comfort Zion and choose Jerusalem as his own."

Job, who was respected and revered in the Hebrew Bible for his faithfulness to God during trials and tribulations, encourages himself. Job recognizes the fact after the death of his children and losing all his livelihood that a man is born of a woman in a few days and full of trouble. He experiences so much hardship that many people in his situation might have considered suicide. Job learns firsthand that not all a person's friends and family members will provide support and words of encouragement. Job's wife suggests to him that he should curse God because his health continues to decline instead of improving. In the words of Job, "At least I can take comfort in this: Despite the pain, I have not denied the words of the Holy One" (Job 6:10). Due to Job's faith in God, he holds on and waits patiently on God's deliverance. Job speaks these words to Eliphaz during his time of suffering:

> I have heard all this before. What miserable comforters you are! Won't you ever stop blowing hot air? What makes you keep on talking? I could say the same things if you were in my place. I could spout off criticism and shake my head at you. But if it were me, I would encourage you; I would try to take away your grief. Instead, I suffer if I defend myself, and I suffer no less if I refuse to speak. (Job 16:1-6)

In many cases, this passage from Job resonates with individuals living with HIV/AIDS. Oftentimes, they become recipients of harsh criticism and condemnation from family, friends, and even members of their own church family. Since this lack of compassion is offered to them, people living with the virus could walk away from the church and from God. What if the church encouraged these individuals to read Job in order to learn how God rewarded Job for his sacrifice, endurance, and, most importantly, his patience instead? God rewarded Job for not turning in the opposite direction but making an attempt to get closer to God during the most challenging time of his life. Job even recognized how the people who he thought would minister to him in time of need were the ones who passed judgment and pleaded for him to repent to God for his sins in order to be healed.

The prophet Isaiah shows God's softer side to the church. While God may give consent to our adversaries to attack us and to have temporary rule over us, God will not permit our rivals to destroy us. We have security in knowing that God hears our prayers and cries. God shows compassion when believers request forgiveness of sins and return to God, the main source of living. When comfort is offered to those who are suffering, a transformation takes place. In this transformation, the receiver obtains the good news that help is on the way, which provides verification that God's favor is present in their lives. Therefore, individuals regain self-confidence and a renewed spirit. They begin to rebuild their lives with a new perspective and with a desire to become witnesses to others.

Many biblical scholars believe that Isaiah's pericope was speaking of a future Messiah who will fulfill this prophecy and not referencing Jesus. Could the scholars be correct in their assumption? The evidence could be found in the Gospel according to Luke when Jesus stood in the synagogue, unrolled the scroll, and recited Isaiah 61:1:

> The Spirit of the Lord is upon me, for he has anointed me to bring Good News to the poor, He has sent me to proclaim that captives will be released, that the blind will see, that the oppressed will be set free, and that the time of the Lord's favor has come."
>
> The Scripture you've just heard has been fulfilled this very day. (Luke 4:18-19, 21)

However, my view is that God had anointed Isaiah to be the anointed one to offer comfort to the children of Israel during those challenging times. Therefore, when Jesus stood in the synagogue and read the scroll, Jesus took the opportunity to confirm his purpose for ministry in the presence of the congregation.

HEALING THE BROKENHEARTED

Both Isaiah and Luke address the main points of comforting the brokenhearted, confirming the church's responsibility and role. The church must recognize the fact that most of its participants may presently be suffering from a broken heart. In most cases, the cause of the broken heart is not because the person to whom they have poured out their souls in love has fallen out of love with them, but worshippers are brokenhearted due to suffering in private for a lack of comfort and emotional support.

Many who believe in God find it difficult to share their deeper feelings with family and friends, so they carry the burden of their issues alone. When they come to the house of worship, they desire to be in a safe place. They hope that, in the house of worship, they can receive an inspiring word, sing an uplifting song of praise, or hear a prayer of supplication, which could mend their broken hearts. Some houses of worship may contain at least one person living with HIV/AIDS who suffers daily in private because they do not have anyone with whom they can share their status and concerns and ask whether they will enter heaven with a positive status of HIV/AIDS. They desire to receive comfort from friends, family, co-workers, and even church members. However, with the continuous judgmental attitudes from others and the stigma associated with the virus, the church continues to remain silent on this subject.

Even the apostle Paul charged churches to offer comfort and support. Romans 15:5-6 says, "May God, who gives this patience and encouragement, help you live in complete harmony with each other, as it is fitting for following Christ Jesus. Then all of you can join together with one voice giving praise and glory to God, the Father of our Lord Jesus Christ." Further, 2 Corinthians 3-7 reads:

> All praises to God, the Father of our Lord Jesus Christ. God is our merciful Father and the source of all comfort.

> He comforts us in all our troubles so that we can comfort others. When they are troubled, we will be able to give them the same comfort God has given us. For the more we suffer for Christ, the more God will shower us with this comfort through Christ. Even when we are weighed down with troubles, it is for your comfort and salvation! For when we ourselves are comforted, we will certainly comfort you. Then you can patiently endure the same things we suffer. We are confident that as you share in our sufferings, you will also share in the comfort God gives us.

Additionally, 1 Thessalonians 5:14 says, "Brothers and sisters, we urge you to warn those who are lazy. Encourage those who are timid. Take tender care of those who are weak. Be patient with everyone." Also, 2 Thessalonians 4:16 says, "Now may our Lord Jesus Christ himself and God our Father, who loves us and by his grace gave us eternal comfort and a wonderful hope, comfort you and strengthen you in every good thing you do and say." In these scripture passages, Paul hits on the main reason why Christians should comfort each other, which is to strengthen the body of Christ. In a similar vein, the hymnodist Thomas Hastings penned these words:

> Come ye disconsolate, where ye languish. Come to the mercy seat, fervently kneel; Here bring your wounded hearts, here tell your anguish: Earth has no sorrow that heav'n cannot heal. Joy of the desolate, light of the straying, Hope of your penitent, fadeless and pure! Here speaks the Comforter, tenderly saying, Earth has no sorrow that heav'n cannot cure.[2]

The beautiful thing about this Christian journey is knowing where to go to find true comfort, and that is in the presence of the Lord. Reading the pericope in Isaiah 61:1, the reader finds joy in the assurance that somebody is present to heal their broken heart. Whether one interprets this passage to mean that the person providing this level of comfort is Isaiah or Jesus Christ, the solace comes from somebody being present during times of trouble. Since God is present in times of trouble, Christians must share this great news with others who are in trouble and even with the ones not known to be in trouble. The good news from this passage of scripture is that help is present. When individuals do not feel the safety of God during times of trouble, they seek safety in the presence of those living the lifestyle of Christian principles and beliefs.

The second Hebrew Bible pericope is Psalm 146:8b, and it states, "The Lord lifts up those who are weighed down." This division of Psalms is labeled as a communal song of thanksgiving, where the writer offers thanksgiving and encourages the worshippers to offer praises unto God. According to Hebrew Bible scholar Michael Coogan, "Song of Thanksgiving psalms consist largely of the expression of gratitude for divine assistance that has been granted and may be either individual or communal, in the latter case as for a military victory or a plentiful harvest."[3]

In Psalm 146:1-2, the writer shares how the Lord will raise and comfort those who are burdened down with life's issues. The awesome news starts in the first verse of this passage: "Praise the Lord, let all that I am praise the Lord. I will praise the Lord as long as I live. I will sing praises to my God with my dying breath." What a declaration and a powerful testimony to offer in the presence of God and to the people:

> As long as I live, I will give honor and reverence to the Lord. Up to the moment when I take my last breath, I will offer the Lord the highest praise. I will lift up praises to the Lord because he provides me with hope and joy. The Lord delivers on every promise, gives justice to the oppressed, food to the hungry, and makes the heavens and the earth. The Lord frees the prisoners and opens the eyes of the blind.

The psalmist makes a personal testimony of thanksgiving unto the Lord for all the bountiful blessings that have been given, sharing why he offers this praise and recognizing that the Lord was present to provide comfort during the most challenging times. During the most challenging times in life, one can find comfort in the presence of the Lord.

Biblical history details how the children of Israel sometimes placed more trust in the hands of human beings and idols as their source of help. When the Israelites failed to follow the covenant and commandments of God, they experienced much heartache. God allowed their enemies to take them into captivity. The Israelites were taken away from their homeland into a strange land where they were used as slaves. God also allowed a famine to fall upon their land, which affected their economy, and several plagues spread throughout the camp, where an entire generation was wiped out. Despite that, the children of Israel knew to call upon the name of the Lord for help. It was during this cry that the people repented from their sins and returned to the covenant of God.

The good news for the people of Israel was God heard their cry for deliverance from the hands of their oppressors. As God delivered them from their oppressive state, their broken hearts were mended, and the presence of God was with them. This same good news that dates back to the sixth and seventh centuries BCE is present in the twenty-first century. God is present to deliver those who are oppressed, release those who are in captivity, heal the brokenhearted, and claim this as the year of the Lord's favor. God uses Isaiah and the writer of Psalm 146 to spread this message to the people who will listen and be ready to hear sound doctrine. The same good news presented to the children of Israel still applies to humankind in the twenty-first century. Wouldn't it be heartfelt for Christians and believers to share this good news of deliverance to those individuals who are living with HIV/AIDS?

Remembering the Least of These

In the New Testament pericope of Matthew 25:31-46, Jesus speaks on the Final Judgment:

> But when the Son of Man comes in his glory and all the angels with him, then he will sit upon his glorious throne. All the nations will be gathered in his presence, and he will separate the people as a shepherd separates the sheep from the goats. He will place the sheep at his right hand and the goats at his left. Then the King will say to those on his right, "'Come, you who are blessed by my Father, inherit the Kingdom prepared for you from the creation of the world. For I was hungry, and you fed me. I was thirsty, and you gave me a drink. I was a stranger and you invited me into your home. I was naked and you gave me clothing, I was sick and you cared for me. I was in prison and you visited me.'" Then these righteous ones will reply, "'Lord, when did we ever see you hungry and feed you? Or thirsty and give you something to drink? Or a stranger and show you hospitality? Or naked and give you clothing? When did we ever see you sick or in prison and visit you?'" And the King will say, "'I tell you the truth, when you did it to one of the least of these my brothers and sisters, you were doing it to me!'" Then the King will turn to those on the left and say, "'Away with you, you cursed ones, into the eternal fire prepared for the devil and his demons. For I was hungry and you didn't feed me. I was thirsty, and you didn't give me a drink. I was a stranger, and you didn't invite me into your home. I was naked and you didn't give me clothing. I was sick and in prison, and you didn't visit me.'" Then they will reply, "'Lord, when did we ever see you hungry or thirsty or a stranger or naked or sick or in prison, and not help you?'" And he will answer, "'I will tell you the truth, when you refused to help the least of these my brothers and sisters, you were refusing to help me.'" And they will go away into eternal punishment, but the righteous will go into eternal life.

This conversation was one of the many that Jesus conducted with his disciples and the multitudes. Many of the listeners and disciples did not realize that Jesus was using these parables as a precursor of his impending crucifixion, meaning that his goal was to prepare his disciples and his followers for what would take place on Judgment Day.

Jesus' analogy of dividing the people like sheep and goats is interesting. In the analogy, eternal life is rewarded to those individuals who practiced the ministry of service to the least of these; eternal death is rewarded to those selfish individuals who failed to assist those who are the least of these. This important statement is often overlooked: "When you have done it to the least of these, you have done it to me." In looking at this statement, these questions are relevant: Who are the least of these? And why are they important? In Matthew, Jesus describes the least of these as those who are hungry, thirsty, naked, sick, a stranger, or a prisoner. These individuals are so important in Jesus' sight because his ministry was based on saving those who are the least, the lost, and the last. The majority of his teachings and healing ministry were amongst the group whom the upper echelon of society had forgotten.

More than two thousand years later, some questions arise for today's church: are we assisting the least of these? Or are we catering to the greater of these? Have we lost focus on the least of these because they do not look like us? Have we reached the pinnacle of success where we are not willing to bring others up with us? Do we not realize that we can become the least of these at any given moment? The prophet Amos describes how the poor are treated:

> You trample the poor, stealing their grain through taxes and unfair rent. Therefore, though you build beautiful stone houses, you will never live in them. Though you plant lush vineyards, you will never drink wine from them. For I know the vast number of your sins and the depth of your rebellions. You oppress good people by taking bribes and deprive the poor of justice in the courts. (Amos 5:11-12)

Whether consciously or unconsciously, believers of the faith continue to trample the poor and oppressed people through self-centered worship and traditions. Has the church become more concerned about its reputation rather than providing ministry to the poor? Does humanity only think of the poor as individuals who are lazy and only seeking a handout? Has society forgotten that the word poor is also defined as the state of being that also reflects an emotional and mental state? Matthew 5:3 says, "God blesses those who are poor and realize their need for him, for the Kingdom of heaven is theirs." This scripture confirms that poverty is more than an economic state of being but also a mental state of being.

Other New Testament scriptures address how a person will be rewarded for caring for the least of these. For instance, Matthew 10:42 says, "And if you give even a cup of cold water to one of the least of my followers, you will surely be rewarded." Finally, Hebrews 6:9-12 states the following:

> Dear friends, even though we are talking this way, we really don't believe it applies to you. We are confident that you are meant for better things, things that come with salvation. For God is not unjust. He will not forget how hard you have worked for him and how you have shown your love to him by caring for other believers, as you still do. Our great desire is that you will keep on loving others as long as life lasts, in order to make certain that what you hope for will come true. Then you will not become spiritually dull and indifferent. Instead, you will follow the example of those who are going to inherit God's promises because of their faith and endurance.

In these passages, offering a cup of water to the least of these fulfills the teachings of Jesus Christ. Kindness to all people should come naturally and not be forced. When people render acts of kindness, it should not be done to obtain recognition, but the act should be performed because it is in the heart of the performer.

The least of these are crying out for help and for comfort in these last and evil days. They are represented in all generational groups. They are present in every auxiliary and ministry work. Some of the least of these are sitting in the pulpit. This is not a cry for empathy, though; it is a cry for emotional support, guidance, and, most importantly, deliverance. The cry from the least of these is a cry for affirmation that they are in the presence of people who will offer biblical reference to mend their brokenness and remind them that God and their church family have not left them.

When will we answer the call from the least of these, or will we continue to hit the ignore button on the phone? Will the separation of the haves and have-nots continue to divide our house of worship? Until we begin to assist the least of these during their challenging times, we take the chance of being rewarded the prize of eternal death, based on the pericope of Matthew 25:31-46. Victory cannot be obtained by the least of these and by the greater of these until a working partnership has been established. What will you do to create a partnership between the religious community and those individuals who are living with HIV/AIDS to ensure they are made aware that victory is there in Christ Jesus?

Reflection Questions

1. As you read this chapter, what were your thoughts regarding the healing of the brokenhearted and speaking deliverance?
2. Can you share a personal story of being healed from a broken heart? How was your heart mended? Did the mending of your brokenhearted come from words of comfort from your pastor, congregation, or worship service?
3. How would you share this chapter with someone who is living with HIV/AIDS? Would sharing the stories of others be helpful?

NOTES

1. Merriam-Webster Dictionary, "Comfort" (Springfield, MA: Gardners Publishers, 2004).
2. Thomas Moore, "Come, Ye Disconsolate, Where'er Ye Languish," Hymnal, https://www.hymnal.net/en/hymn/h/684, accessed December 30, 2015.
3. Michael Coogan, *The Old Testament: A Historical and Literary Introduction to the Hebrew Scriptures* (New York: Oxford University Press, 2006), 464.

CHAPTER EIGHT

THE TRANSFORMING WORD

DURING A revival service, a young teenager entered the building. This individual was not a regular attendee of any worship services, so the young teenager was not sure what to expect from the service. However, she knew that she was dealing with some personal issues, which caused her to be in a sad state most of the time.

What she heard when she arrived surprised her! The music was uplifting and upbeat, and the people offered prayers that resonated with her spirit. However, the young teenager was perplexed by the content of the message from the guest speaker. The speaker emphasized the phrase, "Tonight, you will be transformed. Transformation is available to you. So, claim it in the name of Jesus." The young teenager wanted to know: how would she know if she was transformed?

Transforming Our Understanding

When we use the terms *transformation* and *transformed*, are we explaining what we mean clearly? Are we using these words correctly? Are we effectively applying these terms in our messages? Are we confusing our audiences instead of encouraging them?

The word *transformation* is frequently heard inside the brick-and-mortar walls of church buildings throughout the world. Regardless of religious beliefs and practice, the objective of many worship services, conferences, conventions, retreats, and other special events is designed to be transformative for each participant. How do you measure transformation? What evidence that transformation is taking or has taken place? Who confirms that a transformation has taken place? In the Hebrew Bible days, in order for someone to be released from a medical condition like leprosy or issue of blood, they were required to go to the priest. The priest pronounced healing, granting permission for an individual reentry to the general public. Are there some words that can be spoken that will lift the countenance of an individual who is living with a chronic illness?

In 1 Corinthians 15:54-58, the apostle Paul shares these words of encouragement to the Corinth Church:

> Then, when our dying bodies have been transformed into bodies that will never die, this scripture will be fulfilled: "Death is swallowed up in victory." O death, where is your victory? O death, where is your sting? For sin is the sting that results in death, and the law gives sin its power. But thank God! He gives us victory over sin and death through our Lord Jesus Christ. So, my dear brothers and sisters, be strong and immovable. Always work enthusiastically for the Lord, for you know that nothing you do for the Lord is ever useless.

In this chapter of Corinthians, Paul speaks of how the physical body is filled with corruption and sin, but those who have accepted the Lord Jesus Christ as their Savior can take on the form of Jesus in their bodies. The death and resurrection of Jesus Christ have taken the sting of death from them, as prophesied by Isaiah 25:6-8:

> In Jerusalem, the Lord of Heaven's Armies will spread a wonderful feast for all the people of the world. It will be a delicious banquet with clear, well-aged wine and choice meat. There he will remove the cloud of gloom, the shadow of death that hangs over the earth. He will swallow up death forever! The Sovereign Lord will wipe away all tears. He will remove forever all insults and mockery against his land and people. The Lord has spoken!

Similarly, Hosea 13:14 says, "Should I ransom them from the grave? Should I redeem them from death? O death, bring on your terrors! O grave, bring on your plagues! For I will not take pity on them."

In these passages of scripture, the Lord served death and the grave the notice of defeat. This scripture expresses the work of Jesus in coming down from heaven to save the people from sin and death. The joy that Paul wanted to share with the Corinthian people was that Jesus defeated death and the grave, so as believers of Jesus Christ, we will not experience the sting of death. For Jesus took that burden upon himself on our behalf. Due to the sacrificial act of Jesus, our earthly body, which is defined as corruptible in the biblical text, will be destroyed. At the time of judgment, humanity will take on the form of incorruptible bodies. Paul reminds the church that the cause of death is based on sinful nature that dates back to the fall in the Garden of Eden, but Jesus came down to earth to redeem humanity from our sins.

Victory in Jesus

Now that the bill of sin has been paid in full by Jesus, we can claim victory through God. Christians have the victory over two powerful forces that keep them from having an intimate relationship with God: sin and death. Asking rhetorical questions is a wonderful way of making a strong statement to one's enemies. That is what Paul did when he asked the following questions to death and to the grave: "Where is your sting? O grave, where is your victory?" Remember the grave thought it had claimed victory over Jesus when he died, but Jesus triumphed over the grave on the third day, just as he had spoken to the disciples and to the multitude. With Jesus claiming victory over these powerful forces, believers can also claim victory over these same forces in life.

When the Bible speaks of the word *victory*, the assertion is that victory belongs to God. There are two special features: (1) The Lord's victory is the defeat of his people's enemies. The scriptural reference is 2 Samuel 23:10: "He killed Philistines until his hand was too tired to lift his sword, and the Lord gave him a great victory that day." (2) The Lord's victory is the exercise of holy sovereignty in the course of history.

Many Hebrew Bible passages include the word *victory*. Here are a few examples, although it is not an exhaustive list. Exodus 15:2 records these words, "The Lord is my strength and my song; he has given me victory." Psalm 20:5 reads, "May we shout for joy when we hear of your victory and raise a victory banner in the name of our God. May the Lord answer all your prayers." Psalm 62:1 says, "I wait quietly before God, for my victory comes from him." Psalm 98:3 says, "He has remembered his promises to love and be faithful to Israel. The ends of the earth have seen the victory of our God." Psalm 118:14 says, "The Lord is my strength; he has given me victory."

In the New Testament, we find the word victory in Matthew 12:20, where it reads, "He will not crush the weakest reed or put out a flickering candle. Finally, he will cause justice to be victorious." Later in Romans 8:37, we read, "No, despite all these things, overwhelming victory is ours through Christ, who loved us." Colossians 2:13-15 states:

> You were dead because of your sins and because your sinful nature was not yet cut away. Then God made you alive with Christ, for he forgave all our sins. He canceled the

> record of the charges against us and took it away by nailing it to the cross. In this way, he disarmed the spiritual rulers and authorities. He shamed them publicly by his victory over them on the cross.

Finally, Revelation 5:5 says, "But one of the twenty-four elders said to me, 'Stop weeping! Look, the Lion of the tribe of Judah, the heir to David's throne, has won the victory. He is worthy to open the scroll and its seven seals.'"

When reading these passages of scriptures, the message provides us with a remedy to triumph over trials and tribulations. Therefore, we can stop stressing, and we can start rejoicing that victory is at hand. From how the children of Israel became triumphant over Pharaoh up to the time when America had declared victory over Saddam Hussein, the message that victory is at hand needs to come across the sacred desk from the person who is delivering the word of God. Let them proclaim the acceptable year of the Lord. These words will send an uplifting message to all congregants, especially to those individuals living with HIV/AIDS.

Good News for All God's Children

Earlier, I shared the Hebrew Bible and New Testament scriptural references about the phrase "the least of these" and how it was used in the form of a parable to inform the multitude and the disciples of how God determines who will enter heaven on Judgment Day. The least of these are those who are hungry, sick, thirsty, naked, and imprisoned. Those characteristics are not only based on physical appearance, but these characteristics are applicable to an individual's state of mind.

Since we can also think of the church as a hospital, the church's mission should be to provide the necessary treatment to those individuals who are standing in need of care. The pastor who serves as the attending physician is responsible for providing the proper and effective medication (the word of God) that will bring healing to the least of these. Jesus is clear that when a person mistreats the least of these, they are mistreating him. Believers must remember God created humankind in the image of God. For this reason, God shares the same feelings, success, hurt, pain, challenges, and other emotions as his children do. When Jesus came down to earth, he took on human form and likeness, which allowed him to bridge the gap between man and God. When we become members of the body of Christ, we become a family. Therefore, regardless of our last names, Christians are one big family. As members of the same body, there are times when one member of the body is hurting and suffering pain.

When Christians are hurting and suffering pain, they go to the hospital to relieve the pain, but in many cases, the least of these are not receiving the proper care or comfort from the church. All who have been baptized into the body of Christ have been called to deliver the good news to all people. As Christians share the Gospel with people, the words of God bring comfort. In Micah 6:8, the prophet encourages his listeners by saying, "The Lord has told you what is good, and this is what He requires of you to do what is right, to love mercy, and to walk humbly with your God." Also, the apostle Paul truly sends an excellent message to the church in Galatia by saying, "Whenever we have the opportunity, we should do good to everyone—especially to those in the family of faith" (Galatians 6:10).

The good news offers a new perspective on life to those who are in anguish and sin. A new portrait is painted on the canvas to illustrate hope and that, most importantly, victory belongs to them. All these positive experiences should be a part of the weekly worship experiences of the church. All members should be able to have this type of experience. When this type of experience is offered to all people, then God will say to us on that great Judgment Day, "Well done, thou good and faithful servant" (Matthew 25:21).

The church is responsible for providing the necessary spiritual medication to those who are suffering and in pain, which will help them prevail over their illness. When they have overcome the trials and tribulations, they can declare that victory is theirs. When members are made aware that through Christ, they are victorious, then their attitude will be positive; they will be able to loudly proclaim, "We are more than conquerors" (Romans 8:37). This was the message from the apostle Paul to the Corinthian Church, and this message is still applicable to today. Because of Jesus' death and resurrection, the sting of death and the grave has been defeated.

Members of the religious community (pastors, evangelists, prophets, prophetess, bishops, choir members, deacons, stewards, trustees, culinary arts members, drama ministry, ushers, nurses, and pew members), regardless of denominational polity, race, and gender, have the golden opportunity to exemplify the compassion of Jesus Christ by putting into action the biblical principles of Matthew 7:1: "Do not judge others, and you will not be judged." Also, Matthew 28:19-20 says, "Therefore, go and make disciples of all the nations, baptizing them in the name of the Father and the Son and the Holy Spirit. Teach these new disciples to obey all the commands I have given you. And be sure of this: I am with you always, even to the end of the age." Using the biblical principles instills into the lives of the least of these that Jesus Christ cares for them and desires for them to cast their care upon him.

The Bible should be the foundation of determining what the moral authority is for the church in the twenty-first century. Second Timothy 2:15 states that "who correctly explains the word of truth" should not be ashamed. We apply the Bible throughout teaching, preaching, and sharing the good news of Jesus Christ. Explaining the word of truth will lead to an understanding of how to provide a positive response to individuals who are living with HIV/AIDS without passing judgment on them.

I have shared biblical texts I believe should be the foundation for offering compassion and meeting the spiritual needs of individuals living with an inoperable illness. Throughout his ministry, Jesus Christ always showed compassion to those individuals in need of healing and deliverance. These individuals came to Jesus based on hearing the good news of others being delivered from their afflictions. They walked in faith, hoping that Jesus would dispense healing virtue upon them. It is no different in the twenty-first century; individuals who are living with HIV/AIDS attend church as an act of faith in order to receive healing from God through the preached word from clergy who have been called by Jesus Christ to spread the Gospel.

These individuals are already feeling the wrath of society because of their diagnosis. Many of the individuals' self-esteem is at an all-time low because they must be very selective in sharing their health status with their loved ones, friends, co-workers, and even their church family. In today's society, these individuals can be thought of as among the least of these.

The New Testament text found in Matthew 25:25-40 directly applies to how Jesus says these individuals should be treated and how he will hold his followers accountable for their mistreatment. According to the text, if we do these things unto them, we have done these things unto him. Does the church want to be indicted on charges of neglect and abandonment of the least of these when they stand before God on Judgment Day? Does the church want to be known as a group of hypocrites for not obeying the red letters of the New Testament text? Is the biblical text only used to practice discrimination and show stigmatization? Only the pastor, church leaders, and you can answer these questions.

Reflection Questions

1. How can we, as believers, ensure our words of encouragement are more transformative and nonjudgmental?
2. What other means, beyond using scriptures, can you use to affirm God's love for individuals living with HIV/AIDS?

3. How does this chapter resonate with you? How can you paint a new portrait of transformation to individuals who are living with HIV/AIDS or chronic illness?

CHAPTER NINE

WHERE DO WE GO FROM HERE?

A YOUNG MAN recently relocated to a new city for his employment. The new position was working as the executive director of an agency that provided social services to individuals who were infected with HIV/AIDS. During his first staff meeting, he asked his team, "How are the area religious communities working with us? Do we have any good partnerships with the churches in the area?" "It's hit or miss," one staff member replied. Another staff member agreed, adding, "Some of our clients have had some negative experiences with local congregations." Finally, someone offered, "I suppose our outreach to the faith communities could be a little better." There were murmurs of agreement from all around the table. All staff members affirmed that they needed to extend more outreach to the religious community and establish partnerships. So, the new executive director asked the staff members to provide a list of area clergy with whom he could dialogue.

His staff quickly drew up a list of ten clergy who represented various religious faiths in the community. He reached out to each of them, introducing himself, his role with the agency, and his desire to schedule an appointment. Out of the ten clergy on the list, only three agreed to meet with him. He met with each of them individually, sharing his background, experiences, and the goals of the agency. Two of the clergy thanked him for reaching out and starting the conversation with him. They told the executive director that they would pass along the information to a church staff member, and the staff member would follow up. One pastor was interested in learning more about the agency and wanted to know how he personally could work with the agency to distribute information to the community. "What kinds of services are offered by the agency to help those who are living with the virus?" he asked.

This question caught the executive director off guard. This pastor shared, "I've been living with the virus for more than fifteen years. My last church created a ministry to serve people like me, and I want to start one here, too." The executive director's eyes lit up with joy and excitement. The pastor had described exactly the kind of initiative he wanted to start at the agency. At his last job with a similar agency, the board of directors had rejected the idea of working with the faith community. After the initial conversation between the executive director and the pastor, they found themselves asking, "Where do we go from here?"

Meeting People Where They Are

The late Howard Thurman was a noted mystic and theologian who served as a pastor and a professor. He shared the story of a lady who was a member of his congregation. This lady would attend worship weekly, sitting in the same seat and falling asleep during his sermon. The church building was small, so Thurman had a clear view of every member.

The fact that this woman kept falling asleep during his sermons caused Thurman some anxiety. So, he decided to visit the woman so he could inquire if his message delivery was causing her to go to sleep. When he arrived at her home, she welcomed him and extended warm hospitality, but she also kept herself busy, tidying up around the house as they spoke. Pastor Thurman tried to engage her in conversation while she continued to be a busybody. He wondered how he could capture her attention and what might cause the woman to take a moment of rest to speak with him. He noticed an ashtray sitting on a table. He looked in his coat pocket and found a small piece of paper. He placed the paper inside the ashtray.

Immediately, the woman noticed the item in the ashtray and removed it. He thought, *let me try this again.* He grabbed an item and placed it in the ashtray. Once again, immediately, the woman noticed the item and removed the item. This time, Pastor Thurman grabbed her hand and gently guided her to take a seat on the couch. He asked her to explain why she would nap through his sermons each week. She responded that the worship service hour was the only time that she could get some rest. It was at this moment that inspired Thurman to call interactions like this "meeting at the ashtray level." Thurman describes the ashtray level as, "In religious experience, God meets the individual at the level not only of the individual's needs, but also, in my judgment more incisively, at the level of his residue of God-meaning and goes forward from there."[1] By paying careful attention to the woman's habits and concerns, Howard was able to connect in a meaningful way.

To provide ministry to people who are living with HIV/AIDS, we must be able to meet them at the ashtray level. We need to sit with them in open honesty, taking whatever action necessary to establish clear communication. To achieve that goal, we must seek to understand and learn what they are going through and what their needs are. Here are some questions that can help start the conversation:

1. Where do you feel like you are in the acceptance process when it comes to your diagnosis? The generally accepted stages of grief are denial, anger, bargaining, depression, and acceptance.
2. What about your spiritual walk? How is your spiritual life?
3. Do you feel like your spiritual life and your acceptance process interact? In what ways?
4. What do you feel you need from our church?

After individuals who are living with the virus share their responses, clergy or members of the church can then share words of encouragement, such as these from Charles E. Booth's "Making the Best Out of a Bad Situation" sermon:

> I don't care how difficult it gets, I don't care how dark life becomes, I can do all things through Jesus Christ who strengthens me. In fact, the beauty of our faith is that the darker life gets, the brighter Christ becomes. The more difficult the times are, the more real he is. I can do all things through Jesus who strengthens me. Let man continue in his greed. Let Wall Street require a bailout. Let the automobile industry go to pot. But when it's all said and done, when the smoke finally clears and the dust settles, I will stand because Christ is Alpha and Omega, the Beginning and the End, the First and the Last. So with Christ standing in the worst of times, who will be right by his side, declaring that the Lord will make a way anyhow?[2]

We know that infected individuals are learning how to make the best out of a bad situation every day. Testing positive for HIV antibodies or being fully diagnosed with AIDS can leave one feeling depressed, lonely, fearful of entering a romantic relationship, and scared of dying alone. Individuals who are living with the virus could seek solace and answers to their unanswered questions by attending Sunday worship services and Bible study. The church can support those with HIV/AIDS by offering a ministry of compassion throughout all church programming.

A Ministry Model

This model is intended to address the needs of churchgoers and community members who are living with the virus. First we will identify key areas of daily concern for these people. By identifying their needs, churches will be able to provide the proper services to minister to their needs.

Abraham Maslow was a noted psychologist who proposed that every person has a hierarchy of needs that must be fulfilled to be motivated in life. He believed that individuals who are living a healthy life do so because they have satisfied all their physiological and psychological needs. For this reason, they have fully integrated the components of their personality or self, attaining self-actualization. These ideas set the foundation of the hierarchy of motivation that bears his name.[3] This model is widely used by education and psychological professionals to understand the needs of the people they serve. When we think about how the church can support individuals living with the virus and other chronic illnesses, we should bear in mind Maslow's Hierarchy of Needs. Let's consider the following model as a foundation for creating a ministry model to support individuals who are living with the virus:

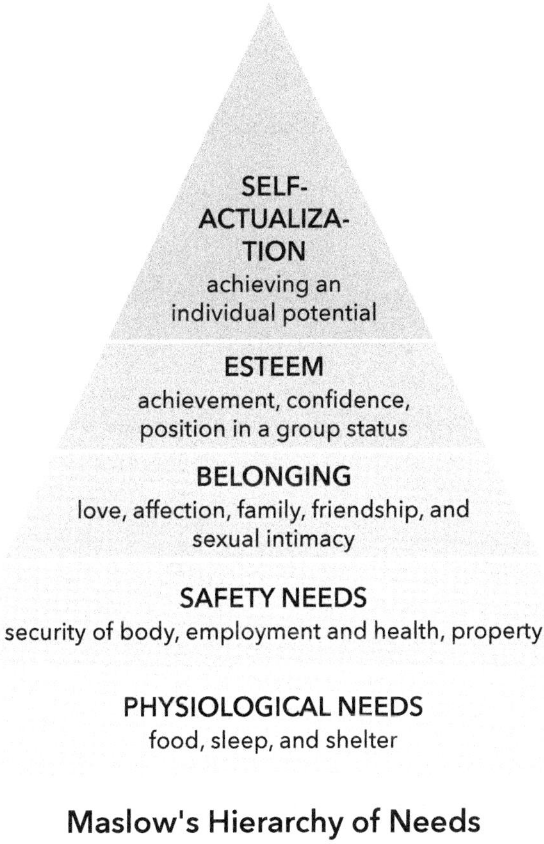

Maslow's Hierarchy of Needs

For a starting point, we can consider how scripture might inform Maslow's Hierarchy. What are some scriptural references that might help support the needs of a person living with HIV/AIDS? For me, the following passages in relation to the hierarchy are helpful for those who are seeking affirmation from God.

1. PHYSIOLOGICAL NEEDS

a. Psalm 46:1—God is my refuge and strength. A very help in times of trouble. This passage of scripture focuses on providing shelter.
b. Psalm 121:3-5—God will not let you stumble; the one who watches over you will not slumber. This passage of scripture focuses on providing sleep.
c. Exodus 16—The entire chapter focuses on providing food.
d. Philippians 4:19—God shall supply all your needs according to God's riches in glory. This passage of scripture focuses on all three areas.

2. SAFETY NEEDS

a. Psalm 27:5—For he will conceal me there when troubles come.
b. Proverbs 1:33—But all who listen to me will live in peace, untroubled by fear of harm.
c. John 10:29—For my Father has given them to me, and he is more powerful than anyone else. No one can snatch them from the Father's hand.
d. 2 Thessalonians 3:3—But the Lord is faithful; he will strengthen you and guard you from the evil one.

3. BELONGING NEEDS

a. John 14:3—When everything is ready, I will come and get you, so that you will always be with me where I am.
b. John 15:7—But if you remain in me and my words remain in you, you may ask for anything you want, and it will be granted!

c. Proverbs 18:24—There are "friends" who destroy each other, but a real friend sticks closer than a brother.
d. Romans 8:28—And we know that God causes everything to work together for the good of those who love God and are called according to his purpose for them.

4. ESTEEM NEEDS

a. Isaiah 26:3—You will keep in perfect peace all who trust in you, all whose thoughts are fixed on you.
b. John 14:27—I am leaving you with a gift—peace of mind and heart. And the peace I give is a gift the world cannot give. So don't be troubled or afraid.
c. Philippians 4:6-7—Don't worry about anything; instead, pray about everything. Tell God what you need and thank him for all he has done.
d. 1 Peter 2:9—But you are not like that, for you are a chosen people. You are royal priests, a holy nation, God's very own possession. As a result, you can show others the goodness of God, for he called you out of the darkness into his wonderful light.

5. SELF-ACTUALIZATIONS

a. Jeremiah 29:11—For I know the plans I have for you, says the Lord. They are plans for good and not for disaster, to give you a future and a hope.
b. Romans 8:37—No, despite all these things, overwhelming victory is ours through Christ, who loved us.
c. Ephesians 3:20—Now all glory to God, who is able, through his mighty power at work within us, to accomplish infinitely more than we might ask or think.
d. Proverbs 16:3—Commit your actions to the Lord, and your plans will succeed.

This is a sampling of scripture that people who are living with HIV may find helpful and that I find personally relevant. What additional examples come to your mind?

In addition to words of scripture, we could also use the following resources and activities to lift their spirits and to impart hope as we better understand individuals' needs:

1. Poetry/positive spoken word
2. Prayer partners
3. Support groups
4. Encouraging writing positive thoughts in a journal

Some people have used the word *hospital* as a metaphor to describe a church. Let's explore that metaphor further. A hospital's purpose is to cure and nurse individuals suffering from illnesses or infirmities. It is vital for patients to be comfortable and feel that they are in a safe space to share with the medical team their symptoms. In some cases, sharing such information is embarrassing and uncomfortable. Oftentimes individuals delay going to a medical facility for fear of being judged for what has caused them to suffer such discomfort. Therefore, it is the friendliness and warmth of the medical team to provide a non-judgmental space where a patient feels at ease. Once the medical team knows the symptoms, then they can proceed with determining a reason for the discomfort and administer a proper treatment, which will relieve the patient from pain and discomfort. Consider what that might mean for people in the life of a church.

How can a church learn how to offer ministry to individuals who are living with HIV/AIDS and other chronic illnesses by thinking of it as a spiritual hospital? Remember, these individuals living with the virus come to church to receive words of hope, to petition God to meet their needs, and to know that during this challenging time in their lives, they can count on their church family for support without judgment. However, for this kind of ministry to take place, churches must be willing to meet people at the ashtray level, so they understand the needs of their fellow churchgoers. These ideas are foundational to establishing an effective HIV/AIDS ministry, which will not only address preventive measures for stopping the virus's spread but also meet the spiritual needs of those who are living with it.

FIRST STEPS IN ESTABLISHING AN EFFECTIVE HIV/AIDS MINISTRY

Rarely are effective ministries the efforts of one person acting alone. To create an effective ministry to support those living with HIV/AIDS, the first step is establishing a team. The process for creating a new team may vary depending on your church's polity and procedures, so you will want to ensure you are working within your established guidelines. You may need to consult with the pastor if you are laity, or you may need to speak with a consistory or board of deacons. Once you are aware of your procedures, I suggest the following steps:

1. Speak with the pastor or appropriate governing body about your desire to establish a small task force to lay the foundation for establishing a ministry of compassion.
2. Ask the pastor to share the idea with the congregation during a Sunday morning worship experience. Perhaps the pastor or another appropriate leader could write an article for the congregation's newsletter or blog.
3. In the announcement, ask for volunteers who would be willing to serve on the task force. Describe the anticipated time requirements and ministry goals so people understand their commitment.
4. Once a group has been formed, have each member share a story of someone who has died from the virus or lived with the virus long-term and how the individual felt alone at the initial meeting.

5. Invite individuals who are living with the virus to come to share their stories and inquire how the church can support them.
6. Invite representatives from the medical and social work fields to share with the task force the mental and physiological challenges that individuals who are living with the virus and chronic illness are dealing with daily.
7. Invite your pastor or other key church leaders to a task force meeting to share your findings and request additional thoughts and ideas.
8. Develop a curriculum plan for your ministry using Maslow's Hierarchy of Needs model.
9. Present the curriculum to the pastor or other appropriate leadership for approval.
10. Ask if the pastor would dedicate a Wednesday evening or Sunday morning Sunday school hour to unveil the curriculum to the congregation.
11. Plan an activity to invite individuals who are living with a chronic illness, which will introduce the new ministry to the church and community. (Examples: meal function, panel discussion, or seminar.)

The mission and objective of this committee is to assist the congregation in affirming the love of God and being a source of refuge and strength to individuals who are living with HIV/AIDS and other chronic illnesses. Another objective of this committee is to guide the church on the path to remove the stigma and dispel the myths that are associated with HIV/AIDS. The committee should share preventative materials and resources on how to stay healthy with congregants. This is only one idea on how to start the conversation in a congregation about providing support to those individuals who are living with HIV/AIDS.

OTHER CONSIDERATIONS

What inspires your ministry? An inspiring theme or motto can help bring together a group or team and unify their work. You might consider using a scriptural passage as a theme for your HIV/AIDS ministry. One such scripture could be 1 Corinthians 15:58: "So, my dear brothers and sisters be strong and immovable. Always work enthusiastically for the Lord, for you know that nothing you do for the Lord is ever useless." This verse could inspire individuals living with the virus to be encouraged in knowing that by the grace and mercy of God, they can shout with a loud voice, "Hallelujah! I am victorious!" You might find other passages equally inspiring. What other passages might you consider as the theme or motto for your ministry? Remember, this ministry is intended to provide hope and encouragement to individuals who are living with HIV/AIDS, and your choice should reflect that purpose. Another important consideration while developing a ministry is that it may prompt the church to have a conversation about sex and how to be comfortable with sexuality. The congregation may need to open their eyes to how they have unknowingly continued the cycle of discrimination against a group of people based on their health status. While religious exclusion was standard in the Hebrew Bible and New Testament for those individuals suffering from leprosy or other blood diseases, this kind of ministry seeks to provide liberation for individuals who are living with HIV/AIDS.

You may find, in the process of creating such a ministry, that you not only bring hope to those living with HIV/AIDS, but you also become more self-understanding and self-compassionate. Pastor Howard Thurman writes, "A person becomes conscious of himself; the urge to know, to understand, to find answers, turns inward. Every estimate of others becomes a question of self-estimate, every judgment upon life becomes a self-judgment. The question of the meaning of oneself becomes one with the meaning of life."[4] As members of the congregation gain knowledge, they become aware of how their lack of compassion and acceptance of people who are infected have caused HIV-positive persons to withdraw from the church and God. The congregation should not desire to push people away from God but to encourage people to proceed to God with all their problems, issues, and cares. To provide a hopeful and healing space for others, we must first find hope and healing within ourselves.

So How Do Churches Change Their Ways and Become Places of Support?

In his book *Healing Our Broken Village,* pastor Frederick D. Hayes III writes, "God is so good that when you walk by faith your consequences will never be limited by your conditions."[5] He reminds us that these words need to be shared with individuals who are living with HIV/AIDS and other chronic illnesses. The church must remind people that God has been so good that God has not allowed your health status to determine your consequences. Once we begin as a church to share this powerful message, the barrier of stigma against HIV/AIDS and other chronic illnesses will come down, and the gates of compassion, love, and affirmation will swing open wide for them to gladly walk through unapologetically into the house of the Lord.

Throughout the ministry of Jesus Christ, he intended to change the hearts, minds, and souls of those who were willing to listen to his message. He focused on a message of hope and words of encouragement that would lift up the countenance of individuals who had been mentally abused, physically exploited, and spiritually discriminated against. As we profess to be Christlike-minded individuals whose goal is to exemplify the persona of Jesus Christ, we must display these tenets with individuals who are living with HIV/AIDS and other chronic illnesses.

My goal in writing this book has been to open the church's eyes to the fact that a group of individuals are suffering in silence and are sending out an SOS message to affirm God's love. These individuals are not seeking self-pity but desire to be included on the prayer list for healing, comfort, restoration of joy, and restored hope. I invite you to continue to dialogue on ways to offer ministry to churchgoers and community members who are walking through life battling chronic illnesses and to respond to the clarion call of healing those who are sick, set the captive free, mind the broken heartedness, and to announce the acceptable year of the Lord. Now is the time to open your heart and ears to what members of your church and community are seeking. We can stop the continuous cycle of ignoring the spiritual and mental well-being of humankind, but we must be willing to hear the voice of those who are crying in the wilderness, because they are daily asking the question, can we talk? Imagine what will happen if you answer the call!

A PARTING STORY

A YOUNG MAN was walking in a neighborhood on a Saturday afternoon when he came across an event being held in a church parking lot. As he came closer, he saw a sign that read, "We're a church that is committed to community by providing services that will meet the needs of members and the community at large." The sign's message captured the young man's attention, and he became interested in learning more about this church. In the parking lot, more than twenty-five vendors were selling things of interest, such as clothing, books, jewelry, art paintings, food, and other items. Several social services agencies were present, distributing materials and offering complimentary health screenings. However, one table captured the young man's eye from a distance—the HIV/AIDS ministry table. As he drew closer to that table, he thought to himself that this table would contain the usual HIV/AIDS prevention information. He thought it was probably going to provide complimentary safe-sex pamphlets and a list of scripture references about how homosexuality and premarital sexual activity is a sin unto God. However, when he reached the table, a man greeted him with a smile. So, the young man asked the man to share more information about this HIV/AIDS ministry.

The man from the HIV/AIDS ministry explained that this was an outreach ministry of the congregation. The ministry was established more than thirty years ago by several mothers whose children had died from AIDS. At the time of these individuals' deaths, this congregation was one of the only churches open to hosting funeral services for people who had died of AIDS or its complications. The pastor at the time felt the need to show compassion to this community of individuals who had been marginalized by a society based on their health status. These mothers made the pastor and congregation aware of how individuals who were living with the virus were in fear of being abandoned and rejected if they shared their status. These mothers shared with the leaders of the church how individuals desire to receive affirmation of God's love and inclusion. After the mothers presented this information, the pastor asked them to take the lead in establishing a more robust ministry to provide spiritual support and affirmation to individuals living with the virus and their families. This is how the church's HIV/AIDS ministry was born. The ministry representative continued to share how the ministry holds group sessions so individuals could have a safe space to share how they were wrestling and coming to grips with their diagnosis. Individuals shared challenging life stories that they had encountered since testing positive and, most importantly, how their family members had accepted or rejected them. He explained to the young man how the ministry leaders were trained as pastoral care counselors to offer words of affirmation, positive reflections, and scripture references to demonstrate the love of God and the acceptance of God.

The young man was extremely impressed with the information from the ministry representative. He asked many questions: Was this printed material to take home? When does this ministry meet? Does an individual have to be a member of the congregation to participate in the ministry? Was there a cost associated with the ministry? The ministry representative responded that the ministry was open to anyone who would like to participate, regardless of their health status or membership with the church. He also shared the day of the week and time when the group meets. The young man was so grateful for the information! He attended the worship service of the church the following day. He also began attending the HIV/AIDS ministry monthly meetings. That following Sunday, the young man joined the church, saying, "I have been seeking a church home where I can feel comfortable and affirmed. I have been living with HIV for a short period of time; however, I felt that God had abandoned me and I felt that the church would reject me, so I made the decision to keep my status to myself. I had an excellent conversation with the ministry representative of the HIV/AIDS ministry and attended one HIV/AIDS ministry session. I feel confident that this congregation is where I need to be."

It only takes one member of a congregation to have the mindset of compassion and step out of traditional modes of offering ministry. Offering a specialized ministry or service to your congregation membership shows that you are concerned not just about their spiritual needs but about their holistic needs. This type of ministry can make a difference and provide a positive outlook on individuals who are in despair and living in darkness. Will you make that difference for someone in your community today?

REFLECTION QUESTIONS

1. What other resources could be included in your church's ministry?
2. After reading this chapter, how might you become involved in forming the task force for your congregation?

3. How does this chapter resonate with you based on your knowledge and experience on the subject of HIV/AIDS?
4. What other biblical reference would you consider adding to the ministry model?

NOTES

1. Howard Thurman, *The Creative Encounter* (Richmond, IN: United Press, 1972), 27.
2. Charles E. Booth, *Stronger in My Broken Places: Claiming A Life of Fullness in God* (Chicago: MMGI Books, 2014), 3.
3. Britannica Biography of Abraham H Maslow, www.britannica.com/biography/Abraham-H-Maslow, accessed November 14, 2024.
4. Howard Thurman, *The Inward Journey* (Richmond, IN: Friends United Press, 1972), 17.
5. Fredrick D. Hayes III, *Healing Our Broken Village* (Dallas: St. Paul Press, 2009), 202.

BIBLIOGRAPHY

Ackermann, Denise M. "Engaging Stigma: An Embodied Theological Response to HIV and AIDS: The Challenge of HIV/AIDS to Christian Theology." *Scriptura* 89 (2005): 385–395.

Adelekan, Tokunbo. *A Charge to Keep: Re-Missioning the Urban Church for the Twenty-First Century.* Chicago: MMGI Books, 2014.

Adler, Michael W. *ABC of HIV and AIDS.* 6th ed., Chichester, UK: Blackwell Publishers, 2012.

Aga, Fekadu, Jari Kylma, and Merja Nikkonen. "Sociocultural Factors Influencing HIV/AIDS Caregiving in Addis Ababa, Ethiopia." *Nursing and Health Sciences* 11, no. 3, (September 2009): 244–51.

Aggleton, Peter, and Richard Parker. *A Conceptual Framework and Basis for Action: HIV/AIDS Stigma and Discrimination.* Geneva, Switzerland: Joint United Nations Programme on HIV/AIDS (UNAIDS), 2007.

Aholou, Tiffany M. Cummings, Jerry E. Gale, and LaTrina M. Slater. "African American Clergy Share Perspectives on Addressing Sexual Health and HIV Prevention in Premarital Counseling: A Pilot Study." *Journal of Religion and Health,* vol. 50. (2011): 330–347.

Akbar, Na'im. *Breaking the Chains of Psychological Slavery.* Tallahassee: Mind Productions and Associates, 1996.

Alexander, Michelle, and Cornel West. *The New Jim Crow: Mass Incarceration in the Age of Colorblindness.* New York: New Press, 2012.

Ammerman, Nancy. *Congregations and Community.* New Brunswick, NJ: Rutgers University Press, 2001.

Bandy, Thomas. *Moving Off the Map: Your Church Can Reach New People.* Nashville: Abingdon Press, 1998.

Barna, George. *The Habits of Highly Effective Churches.* Ventura, CA: Regal Books, 1999.

Bartlett, John G., and Ann K. Finbeiner. *The Guide to Living with HIV Infection Developed at Johns Hopkins AIDS Clinic.* 6th ed., Baltimore: Johns Hopkins University Press, 2007.

Bate, Stuart C. "Good News for AIDS Myths." *Missionalia,* vol. 30. (2002): 93–108.

Beckman, Nancy L. *Couples of Mixed HIV Status: Clinical Issues and Inventions.* New York: Haworth Press, 2005.

Blackaby, Henry, Richard Blackaby, and Claude King. *Experiencing God: Knowing and Doing the Will of God.* Nashville: B and H Publishing Group, 2008.

Blyther-Smith, Ida, Annette Y. Fields, and Angel D. Jones. *A Woman's Story: Overcoming the Shame of HIV.* Homewood, IL: Kingdom Publishing, 2005.

Booth, Charles. *Stronger in My Broken Places: Claiming a Life of Fullness in God.* Chicago: MMGI Books, 2014.

Brown, Marvelyn, and Courtney Martin. *The Naked Truth: Young, Beautiful and (HIV) Positive.* Nashville: HarperCollins Books, 2008.

Brown, Olou. *Zero-80: Innovative Ideas for Planting and Accelerating Church Growth.* Atlanta: Impact Press, 2010.

Burnett, Miriam J. "How the Black Church May Advance Health and Wholeness in Response to the HIV/AIDS Pandemic in African-Americans." *Journal of the Interdenominational Theological Center, vol.* 35, no. 1-2. (Fall-Spring 2007-08): 173–181.

Butler, Lee H. *Liberating Our Dignity, Saving Our Souls.* St. Louis: Chalice Press, 2006.

Byamugsha, Gideon B. *Church Communities Confronting HIV/AIDS.* London: SPCK, 2010.

Campolo, Tony. *Red Letters Christians: A Citizen's Guide to Faith and Politics.* Ventura, CA: Regal, 2008.

Chan, Jennifer. *Politics in the Corridor of Dying: AIDS Activism and Global Health Governance.* Baltimore: Johns Hopkins University Press, 2015.

Cohen, Mary Ann. *Handbook of AIDS Psychiatry.* New York: Oxford University Press, 2010.

Cone, James H. *God of the Oppressed.* Maryknoll, NY: Orbis Books, 1997.

Cone, James H., and Wilmore, Gayraud S. *Black Theology: A Documentary History,* vol. 1, 1966–1979. Maryknoll, NY: Orbis Books, 1993.

———. *Black Theology: A Documentary History.* Vol. 2. 1980–1992. Maryknoll, NY: Orbis Books, 1993.

Cordeiro, Wayne. *The Irresistible Church: Twelve Traits of a Church Heaven Applauds.* Minneapolis: Bethany House, 2011.

Croom, Emma Y. "A Response to 'Lift Up Your Voice Like a Trumpet!' Mobilizing African-American Churches to Respond to the HIV/AIDS Pandemic." *Journal of the Interdenominational Theological Center*, vol. 35, no. 1-2. (2008): 259–263.

Davis, Harold D. *Can I Call You Solider?* Chicago: Moody Press, 2006.

Derose, Kathryn Pitkin. *The Role of Faith-Based Organizations in HIV Prevention and Care in Central America.* Santa Monica, CA: Rand Publishers, 2010.

Doyal, Lesley, and Len Doyal. *Living with HIV and Dying with AIDS Diversity, Inequality and Human Rights in Global Pandemic.* Farnham Surrey, UK: Ashgate, 2013.

Ellis, Larry W. *Sermon Notes*, vol. 2. Dallas: St. Paul Press, 2010.

Frank, Thomas Edward. *The Soul of the Congregation: An Invitation to Congregational Reflection*: Nashville: Abingdon Press, 2000.

Fuller, Oveta. "Breaking the Silence: A Science-Based Intervention that Empowers Faith Leaders to Address Challenges of HIV/AIDS." *Journal of the Interdenominational Theological Center*, vol. 35, no. 1-2. (Fall-Spring 2007–08): 191–202.

Garcia-Rodriguez, Rosalia. *Investing in Communities Achieves Results: Findings from an Evaluations of Community Responses to HIV/AIDS.* Washington, DC: World Bank, 2013.

Geary, Adam M. *Antiblack Racism and the AIDS Epidemic: State Intimacies.* New York: Palgrave Macmillan, 2014.

Gibbs, Eddie. *Emerging Churches: Crafting Christian Community in Postmodern Cultures.* Grand Rapids, MI: Baker Academic, 2005.

Gifford, Allen L., Kate Lorig, Diana Laurent, and Virginia Gonzalez. *Living Well with HIV and AIDS*, 3rd ed. Boulder, CO: Bull Publishing Company, 2005.

Gilbert, Dorie, J. and Ednita M. Wright. *African-American Women and HIV/AIDS: Critical Responses.* Westport, CT: Praeger, 2003.

Gould-Champ, Patricia A. "The Black Church in the Era of HIV/AIDS: What is Our Testimony? What is Our Legacy?" *Journal of the Interdenominational Theological Center*, vol. 35, no. 1-2. (Fall-Spring 2007–08): 183–189.

Grab, Wilheim, Lars Charbonnier, and Mary Elizabeth Moore. *Secularization Theories, Religious Identity and Practical Theology:*

Developing International Practical Theology for the Twenty-First Century. Piscataway, NJ: Berlin Lit, 2009.

Griffin, Darrell. *Navigating Pastoral Leadership: In the Transition Zone "Arriving in the Middle of the Movie."* Chicago: MMGI Books, 2012.

Gutierrez, Gustavo. *A Theology of Liberation: History, Politics, and Salvation*. Maryknoll, NY: Orbis Books, 1973.

Haddad, Bev. *Religion and HIV and AIDS: Charting the Terrain*. Scottsville Pietermaritzburg, South Africa: University of Kwazulu-Natal Press, 2011.

Harris-Lacewell, Melissa Victoria. *Barbershops, Bibles and BET: Everyday Talk and Black Political Thought*. Princeton, NJ: Princeton University Press, 2004.

Hauerwas, Stanley, and William Willimon. *Resident Aliens*: *Life in the Christian Colony*. Nashville: Abingdon Press, 2014.

Haug, Kari Storstein. "Overcoming HIV/AIDS-Related Stigmatization and Affirming Life in the African Context: The Role of Theology." *Svensk Missionstidskrift* 97, no. 2. (2009): 211–227.

Hayes, Frederick D., III. *Healing Our Broken Village*. Dallas: Saint Paul Press, 2008.

Hendricks, Howard G., and William D. Hendricks. *Living by the Book*. Chicago: Moody Press, 1991.

Hodge-Wright, Maris E. *Life Lessons: Stories of Hope, Love and Laughter in the Face of AIDS*. Lincoln, NE: iUniverse, Inc., 2004.

Igo, Robert. *Listening with Love: Pastoral Counseling: A Christian Response to People Living with HIV/AIDS*. Geneva, Switzerland: World Council of Churches, 2005.

Jenkins, Carolyn. *Preaching with AIDS: The Carolyn Jenkins Story*. Bloomington, IN: AuthorHouse, 2006.

Jones, Mary S. *It's Personal: HIV/AIDS Real Stories about Real People: The Day the Ground Fell Under Me*. Bloomington, IN: AuthorHouse, 2008.

Jones, Michael K. *Abundant Relationships: The Path to an Amazing Life Promised by God*. Maitland, FL: Xulon Press, 2012.

Karpf, Ted. *Restoring Hope: Decent Care in the Midst of HIV/AIDS*. New York: Palgrave Macmillan, 2008.

Lincoln, E. Eric, and Mamiya Lawrence. *The Black Church in the African American Experience*. Durham, NC: Duke University Press, 1990.

Lopez, Ian Henry. *Dog Whistle Politics: How Coded Racial Appeals Have Reinvented Racism and Wrecked the Middle Class.* Oxford, NY: Oxford University Press, 2014.

Mackenzie, Sonja. *Structural Intimacies Sexual Stories in the Black AIDS Epidemic.* New Brunswick, NJ: Rutgers University Press, 2013.

McCorn, Lester A. *Standing on Holy Common Ground*: Chicago: MMGI Books, 2013.

McCree, Donna Hubbard, Kenneth T. Jones, and Ann O'Leary. *African Americans and HIV/AIDS: Understanding and Addressing the Epidemic.* New York: Springer, 2010.

Melbourne, Bertram. "End the Silence." *Journal of the Interdenominational Theological Center,* vol. 35, no. 1-2 (Fall-Spring 2007–08): 229–239.

Minor, Stephany D. *Fear Near, Believe Only: Miracles Received Throughout My Journey Having HIV/AIDS.* Hampstead, MD: Old Line Publishing, 2013.

Mitchell, Henry H., and Thomas M. Emil. *Preaching for Black Self-Esteem.* Nashville: Abingdon Press, 1994.

Moore, Thomas. "Come, Ye Disconsolate, Where'er Ye Languish." As altered by Thomas Hastings. Accessed December 30, 2015. https://www.hymnal.net/en/hymn/h/684.

Obama, Barack. *The Audacity of Hope:* New York: Three Rivers Press, 2006.

O'Leary, Ann. *Beyond Condoms: Alternative Approaches to HIV Prevention.* New York: Kluwer Academics/Plenum Publishers, 2002.

Osaigbovo, Rebecca Florence. *It's Not About You: It's About God.* Downers Grove, IL: IVP Books, 2003.

Pequegnat, Willo, and Carl C. Bell. *Family and HIV/AIDS Cultural Contextual Issues in Prevention and Treatment.* New York: Springer, 2012.

Price, Frederick K. C. *Race, Religion and Racism.* Vol. 1. *A Bold Encounter with Division in the Church.* Los Angeles: Faith One Publishing, 1999.

Price, Frederick K. C. *Race, Religion and Racism.* Vol 2. *Perverting the Gospel to Subjugate a People.* Los Angeles: Faith One Publishing, 2001.

Price, Frederick K. C. *Race, Religion and Racism.* Vol. 3. *Jesus, Christianity and Islam.* Los Angeles: Faith One Publishing, 2002.

Rankin, Nancy. *Checking Vital Signs: Assessing Your Local Church Potential.* Graham, NC: Plowpoint Press, 2011.

Roberts, Robin. *Everybody's Got Something.* New York: Grand Central Publishing, 2014.

———. *From the Heart: Seven Rules to Live By.* New York: Hyperion, 2007.

Rognlien, Bob. *Experiential Worship: Encountering God with Heart, Soul, Mind and Strength.* Colorado Springs: NavPress, 2005.

Rothschild, Joe. *Hope: A Story of Triumph.* Charlottesville, VA: Hampton Roads Publishing, 2002.

Schuller, Robert H. *Tough Times Never Last, But Tough People Do!* New York: Bantam Books, 1984.

Sims, Darryl D. *The Burden Bearer: Seventeen Messages of Hope and Healing for Black Men.* Chicago: MMGI Books, 2011.

Skjegstad, Joy F. *7 Creative Models for Community Ministry.* Valley Forge, PA: Judson Press, 2013.

Smith, J. Alfred. *On the Jericho Road: A Memoir of Racial Justice, Social Action and Prophetic Ministry.* Downers Grove, IL: InterVarsity Press, 2004.

Smith, J. Alfred, and Berndt Brooks. *Sounding the Trumpet: How Churches Can Answer God's Call to Justice.* Boiling Springs, NC: A Pair of Docs Publishing, 2013.

Sommerville, Raymond R., Jr. "'Lift Up Your Voice Like a Trumpet!' Mobilizing African-American Churches to Respond to the HIV/AIDS Pandemic." *Journal of the Interdenominational Theological Center,* vol. 35, no. 1-2 (2008): 247–257.

Spong, John Shelby. *Living in Sin? A Bishop Rethinks Human Sexuality.* San Francisco: HarperCollins Publishers, 1990.

Stetzer, Ed. *Comeback Churches: How 300 Churches Turned Around and Yours Can Too.* Nashville: B and H Publishing, 2007.

Stevenson, Jerome. *Mentoring Men: A Manual for Men.* Bloomington, IN: Westbow Press, 2014.

Stewart, Carlyle Fielding, III. *The Empowerment Church.* Nashville: Abingdon Press, 2001.

Strong, James. *The Exhaustive Concordance of the Bible.* Nashville: Thomas Nelson Publishers, 1996.

Thomas, Frank A. *The Choice.* Chicago: MMGI Books, 2013.

———. *They Like to Never Quit Praisin' God.* Cleveland: The Pilgrim Press, 2013.

Thompson, Alfred L. *Bars, Bridges and Blessings: A Three-Dimensional Theory for Your Success*. Maitland, FL: Xulon Press, 2015.

Thompson, George B., Jr. *Alligators in the Swamp*. Cleveland: The Pilgrim Press, 2005.

Thurman, Howard. *The Creative Encounter*. Richmond, IN: Friends United Press, 1972.

———. *The Inward Journey*. Richmond, IN: Friends United Press, 1972.

———. *Jesus and the Disinherited*. Boston: Beacon Press, 1996.

Weatherford, Ronald Jeffrey, and Carole Boston Weatherford. *Somebody's Knocking at Your Door: AIDS and the African American Church*. Binghamton, NY: The Haworth Pastoral Press, 1999.

Weems, Lovett H., Jr. *Take the Next Step: Leading Lasting Change in the Church: Discoveries Insights for Church Leadership*. Nashville: Abingdon Press, 2003.

Whelchel, Henry, Jr. *Hell without Fire: Conversion in Slave Religion*. Nashville: Abingdon Press, 2002.

White, James R. *Pulpit Crimes: The Criminal Mishandling of God's Word*. Birmingham, AL: Solid Ground Christian Books, 2006.

Williams, C. Dennis. *An Ecclesiastical Model for HIV/AIDS Ministry*. Bloomington, IN: Author House, 2010.

Young, G. Martin. *Insanity of Theology: God-Talkers Dressed with Inner Vestments*. Chicago: MMGI Books, 2014.

———. *Zechariah's Visions in the Night*. Atlanta: JJG Publishing, 2012.